# Fast Track

# Fast Track

The Superachievers and
How They Make It to Early
Success, Status and Power

## by Mary Alice Kellogg

McGraw-Hill Book Company

NEW YORK   ST. LOUIS   SAN FRANCISCO   DÜSSELDORF
MEXICO   TORONTO

Book design by Mary Brown.

1 2 3 4 5 6 7 8 9 0 B P B P 7 8 3 2 1 0 9 8

Library of Congress Cataloging in Publication Data

Kellogg, Mary Alice.
Fast track.
Includes index.
1. Success.    2. Young adults.    I. Title.
HF5386.K27    650'.1    78-9091
ISBN   0-07-033507-9

*For Katherine, whose path to success was interrupted
to give me life and independence.*

*For Ava, whose friendship gives me courage.*

*For Michael, because I promised.*

# Acknowledgments

MORE THAN seventy people gave of their time and knowledge in the researching of this book. I am thankful to each of them. For their generosity and great good sense, I am especially grateful to Professor Eugene Emerson Jennings of Michigan State University, Ray Hickok, founder of the Young President's Organization, and Peter H. Engel, president of Helena Rubinstein, Inc., overachievers all.

Thirty-five young achievers gave of themselves for the long, gut-level interviews and inevitable follow-ups that constitute an important part of this book. Their willingness to share their hopes and fears is deeply appreciated. Their candor—and vulnerability—gave me invaluable insights into a many-faceted phenomenon.

To Merri Rosenberg, my research assistant, goes a special note of thanks. Her diligent fact-finding, perception and unfailing enthusiasm for this book made it impossible to lose faith. Her contribution to the book cannot be minimized.

The support system needed for a project this size incorporates not only professional sources, but also personal life-lines. I owe a great debt to those friends who believed in it as much as I did, and believed in me even more. For their encouragement, thanks be to Helga Charnes, the women of Dialogue, Ardy Hoeke and Marilyn Salenger. Special appreciation must go to Terri Schultz, who shared so unselfishly her authorship experiences that I might be spared some of the pitfalls of publishing, and to my agent, Timothy Seldes, who helped make my maiden voyage a positive experience.

# CONTENTS

# Introduction:
# Who's Making It Young

THE IDEA OF becoming successful in America while young is not peculiar to this generation. Perhaps it is calming to realize that the concept of youth taking over the world is not a new one. It happened before, a long time ago. America was founded by young people with the vision, indignation and idealism of their years. They were successful young because they had to be. Thomas Jefferson was 33 when he wrote the Declaration of Independence; John Adams, a curmudgeon of 41. The median age of the signers of the Declaration was 36, with James Madison, at 26, the youngest member of the Continental Congress. Had these people been older—and thereby possibly more conservative, exercising the caution that often comes with age—it's probable that the United States would have taken longer to emerge. Or perhaps the country would have stayed under Britain's rule, and today its citizens would be singing "God Save the Queen" at cricket matches.

Impatience, and the acceptance of the necessity for risk so characteristic of youth throughout the ages, made the Colonies free and independent states. Given the short life expectancies of people in the Colonies, George Washington at 44 was considered an elder statesman and Thomas Jefferson at 33 may have been viewed as slightly more than middle-aged. Yet, throughout our history there have always been those few outstanding individuals who became prominent in their fields long before their peers would dare dream of such achievement. In retrospect we think of such people as old, but while they may have been mature in accomplishment, they were still young in years. In the 1840s, the helm of what is now Citibank was taken over by Moses Taylor, a man still in his early thirties. Robert Maynard Hutchins was named to the presidency of the University of Chicago in 1929, when he was just 30. That institution needed the innovation, the risk-taking that Hutchins' intelligent youth possessed. He had, perhaps, an adventure-someness that had been homogenized out of those who would have been considered the "proper" age. Horatio Alger tales of the young man who through perseverance and hard work built an empire while still in his twenties abound from decade to decade.

But something has changed, and it has changed in our life-time. Never before in our country's history have so many young people held and exercised so much power as today. Never before have the young—via their own impetus or that of circumstance —been catapulted into so many important positions in busi-ness, industry, finance, academia, the law. Our young are "getting there" faster, at speeds that would have boggled another genera-tion. A glance at the daily newspaper confirms it; every day, it seems, there's another example of someone young zooming to the top. A network appoints a 28-year-old as the youngest vice president in its history. A 38-year-old is voted president of a Fortune 500 company. Two reporters—ages 28 and 29—crack the Watergate scandal wide open and become rich in the bargain. Another reporter wins the coveted Pulitzer Prize at 23. Companies announce appointments of executives who are fifteen to twenty years younger than their business equals. A 25-year-old woman handles a $2-billion account on Wall Street. Another major network announces the appointment of a 30-year-old woman as its corporate treasurer. A month later, we read that a 25-year-old woman has succeeded a 50-year-old man as president of a large retail store chain.

In 1967, *Rolling Stone* magazine was founded by a 22-year-old to reflect the tastes of his generation. By 1977, its circulation was more than a half million and its 33-year-old publisher was hailed as the youngest publisher of a major American magazine. That is challenged in early 1978, as *Saturday Review* appoints a 32-year-old publisher. In Washington, a 26-year-old pulls down $48,500 in salary as a deputy press secretary to the President. The President's two top advisers at his Inauguration are 34 and 32. "I don't feel guilty making what I'm making," one White House staffer is quoted as saying, "but I can understand why people think someone in his early twenties shouldn't be earning so much." A 33-year-old woman lawyer is appointed Deputy Counsel of the Army. At 28, she had been part of the Watergate prosecution team and had soared to national prominence. Less visibly, more than a dozen major corporations have, during the last four years, named new chief executives in their thirties and early forties.

We read these accounts—many of them written by young people—with surprise, curiosity and a feeling of creeping senility. We hear and see such people exercising their power via television; the newscaster in many cases is a 24-year-old making $60,000 a year and up. What has happened? What does it all mean? Have we thrown over age and its implied substance for the cosmetic energy and flashy appearance of the young, perhaps at the expense of stability in our institutions?

These questions become more answerable in the light of America's tradition of success. European child prodigies aside, America invented the self-made, successful youth on a grand scale. To make it young and big has always been as All American as General Motors and hot dogs. Yet it took nearly two hundred years, a birth explosion, an unpopular war, a sexual revolution and the expression of the cockiness of youth in a powerful political way to bring us back to the concepts of our original founding, the roots of our success ethic. Through our vocal young, who not only shaped our consciousness during the Sixties but who years after made it big and fast within the system they were thought to have so thoroughly despised, we have come back to the pioneer values of self-determination.

It is difficult to ascertain statistically the precise extent to which the under-40 generation holds power. The Bureau of Labor Statistics, the Small Business Administration, the American Management Association, *Fortune* magazine with its statistics on the top 500 U.S. corporations—all those bodies that chart, plot and dissect America's business and economic lifeblood—do not break down their findings by age. There are simply no overall statistics to compare the number of young people in top or near-top positions in business, finance, law, academia, publishing, and other professions, to those of, say, twenty-five years ago. There are numbers, for instance, to show how far women and minority groups have come in their quest for employment equality and economic parity, but none tell how old the parties are. There are no breakdowns of the myriad groupings by age, an oversight that could be a costly demographic mistake.

Still, there are some measures that give a reasonably clear statistical indication that the young have made tremendous gains in all areas of American life. In academia, for instance, there has been a steady decline in the age level of tenured professors. The colleges and universities, in the past a battlefield for a generation's struggle to express itself and change the system, now find the young making important gains. By 1970, the end of the years of campus unrest, the average age of tenured faculty at Columbia University had already declined an average of three years from two decades before. At Yale University in 1974, the average age at tenure was 39.7 years. In 1977 it was 37.5. Harvard, the nation's oldest university, now lists its average tenure age as a tender—and precise—34.755 years. On the elementary and secondary school levels, teachers were also getting younger. The National Education Association, who pinpointed the median age of teachers in 1961 to be 41 years, has seen a steady decline to 35 in 1971 and a 1977 low of 33.

Such a rush of young people to positions of responsibility has also been reflected in the business community. Fifteen years ago, the median age of executives attending advanced management programs at the University of Southern California was 48. The organizers of these prestigious courses for top executives would not consider an applicant under the age of 38. Those chosen by their companies to attend the programs were thought to be top candidates for running the company; being selected implied a vote of confidence in the executives' business acumen, maturity, judgment and potential. Only the crème de la crème were tapped to go. But as early as 1975, that began to change, not in terms of standards, but in terms of age. In that year the median age of those attending the programs was lowered to 43, and all applicants, regardless of age, were being duly considered. Many of those younger than 38 made it in, and today it is not unusual to see several 30-year-old participants. Other advanced management programs at other universities report similar declines in age level.

All professions are affected. The age of law partners seems to be getting younger. Investment firms and banks are now considering younger men and women for partnerships and high middle-management positions. Publishing houses note a drop in the age level of those holding top editorial jobs.

The under-40 generation is making big inroads and is positioning itself to take over the reins of power. And it expects to take over those reins sooner, rather than later.

Youth and success and power are hard words to pin down. They are relative terms. To define the term "success," in whatever space allocated, is like trying to define love in twenty-five words or less. To attempt to define youth is even more dangerous. In a country that practically invented the success ethic, what does it mean to be successful young? By what measure—whose measure—is someone possessed of both youth and extraordinary accomplishment? Our idea of what success is changes constantly, as our society changes. Once, success was thought to be the exclusive property of Caucasian males. Once, success was measured in absolute terms: money, possessions and position. But the Sixties came along and in many ways changed that. Given the altered states of consciousness that were the outgrowths of that turbulent time, coupled with the intense questioning and soul-searching borne of the civil rights and women's movements, we began to examine our measures of achievement and happiness. It became difficult to say with certainty that a young man who dropped out and moved to rural America to manufacture candles, a young man who lives a spare but content life, is not successful. The shades of gray had been forever etched on a black-and-white consciousness. Could we still label an ambitious man or woman who has climbed the corporate ladder and has become relatively rich while at the same time being personally miserable truly successful? As for youth, could we call "young" a sixteen-year-old boy who must work constantly in his off-school hours to supplement a poor family's income, a boy whose life is filled with budgets and bills instead of baseball? Who says that a 50-year-old woman, whose mind is even more flexible and open to change and full of wonder than that of someone thirty years her junior, is old? It is a subjective field, this definition of youth and success, and it is thick with pitfalls and posturing. Definitions of youth and success, like those of love, are to be found in the eye of the beholder.

Yet concepts of young/old, success/failure must be studied within some structure. So it is my structure, my definitions that form the boundaries. The structure, the definitions, are bent to suit the highly individual subject matter with which this book deals. Those who appear here were chosen because they fit certain criteria. For our purposes, they are termed young successes because they attained a level of responsibility or achievement normally held by someone fifteen to twenty years their senior. Most are under 35; the oldest is 39. They are "young" relative to those around them who hold similar positions or accomplishment and who are in large number much older. For some of those profiled, success implies having a large salary—entrepreneurs who made millions while still in their twenties, lawyers and businesspeople who command top fees. "Rich" is also a relative term. None of those profiled is starving, but neither do the majority have mansions and Rolls-Royces on twenty-four-hour call. For others, position is success—the youngest executive vice president in a major company's history, the youngest college president in the United States. To be a young corporate officer, although not pulling down the money of a young entrepreneur, still does not diminish the importance of the position. While money may be important to many profiled here, it was not the absolute measure of accomplishment. Responsibility and achievement are equally crucial factors.

Power, in the final analysis, separates the bright young overachievers in America today from the bright young average achievers. And like youth, success and love, power is an amorphous term, open to interpretation. Many young achievers have power in the corporate sense; as presidents of their own or someone else's company, they set policy and have their company's resources to back them up. Some achievers we will meet not only have power in their own sphere of work, but influence

outside it, such as one law professor whose private practice takes
him all over the world on matters of international political and
sociological delicacy, or a young businessman who dabbles in
political king-making on the side in his home state. Some are
considered powerful simply because of age. They are in positions
within their companies or law firms or universities or publishing houses that are normally occupied by much older men
or women.

As a group, do these young successes have power? As we
will see later, their generation has vast economic impact. Yet
one trademark of these young successes—and their generation
—is that they do not exercise power or economic impact as a
group. The achievers are as politically diverse and individualistic
as the rest of the population. Some are political and social
activists, using their positions to wield influence, contributing
contacts, expertise and money to causes and candidates in the
spirit of the Sixties. Some sit on corporate boards, using the
influence their position implies, an influence that is heightened
in some ways—as well as complicated—by the fact that they
are usually much younger than other board members. Other
achievers simply do their jobs, which are considerable, working
within their own companies, firms, organizations, universities.
As a group they do not wield power per se. But as individuals
in powerful positions, or positions near the seat of power previously not attainable for one of tender corporate or academic
years, they do have an impact. They are more visible because
they are young, and older colleagues—rightly or wrongly—look
to them to explain the idiosyncrasies of an economically powerful and culturally influential generation. The fact that they are
bank, university and business presidents, lawyers or financiers
close to partnership, editors, writers and agents makes them
inherently powerful. They are in positions to implement policy
and to change it.

The power of the under-40 generation is a new kind of

power. Its impact is in the example of the individuals. How they did it, who they are, how they are changing our businesses and culture and what we can learn from a phenomenon no longer possible to ignore, is what this book is about. We will see who among a bright generation made it big—and fast. We'll examine how they got there, their motivations, backgrounds, and steps to success. We'll see what traits they have that most of us share, and which traits make them special. The impact of the young successes in America today is a large one. The under-40 generation has already changed our cultural and social climates in many ways. Now those members of that generation who are in power are changing the way we do business. They are also changing the institutions we work for and the way we work for those institutions. We'll see how superachievers handle their power differently from previous generations, and we'll learn who feels threatened and what they do about it. We'll learn of the special problems young successes have and how their solutions can help us to cope.

To understand the phenomenon of early achievement is to understand where America is economically, socially and culturally, and where America is heading.

# 1 ☰ Success and the Good Times / Bad Times Generation

WE ARE a youth culture. Yet for years, while we replicated youth in dress and speech, in recreation and viewpoint, we denied them their idealism. Talented young businessmen (women and minorities were rare) were held back for years in jobs they had outgrown. To climb the corporate ladder, it was necessary to spend laborious amounts of time on each rung, for only with age could come the foresight and stability to survive at the top and run the business efficiently. While youth was to be emulated in society, imitated and restored in the offices of plastic surgeons, it was to be restrained in its ambitions. That was its place, after all. Youth was not to be trusted. Only an investment of age and the accumulated experience and wisdom that came with it could return a success dividend. While adults played with hula hoops, bebopped in secret and listened to their children's favorite recording stars on the sly, they would not grant their young the desire for success and ambition the society had fostered in them.

The young, on the other hand, wanted in, and wanted in quickly. But the doors to power were seemingly closed. It was necessary to spend years serving apprenticeships, paying dues, and keeping mouths shut in order to learn. For decades the young did just that, playing the "earn your stripes" game, while being capably anxious to do more.

But during the Sixties, that began to change. We began to give, in some cases under duress, the power that youth had said all along it wanted and could handle. We did that out of exasperation, boredom—and hope, that the young could change the things we and our parents before us had not. But that power was not merely given. It was grabbed as well, by the young who were impatient to have it. They were unwilling to wait around an extra twenty years to enjoy its benefits, struggle with its headaches. We then turned to our young—our clamoring, loudmouthed, self-righteous young—for the answers we had never been able to formulate. The young said they had the answers. We hoped against hope they did, for we certainly did not. The young rode in on an advantageous mix of politics, population and consciousness-raising. They were seasoned with more than a goodly dollop of crisis, turbulence and crashing disillusionment with our society, the running of its institutions, the conducting of its battles, the treatment of its people. We came curiously to youth's doorstep for the answers. Remember when we were their age? We had some answers, but they were fuzzy now, lost in a sea of bills, responsibility, reality. Maybe if we dressed like them we'd remember. Maybe if we talked like them. Maybe if we got rid of our wrinkles and slept around a little in the interests of free love it would come back to us. It didn't. We had to come back to them.

Half a century ago we unconsciously began to lay the foundation that would bring us back to the frontier spirit of acquiescing power to our children. It began during the unfortunate years of the Depression, when the American people of necessity produced the first generation in the nation's history in which the number of births declined. In 1929, only 2.58 million babies were born (almost 3 million, in contrast, had been produced in 1915). Uncertainty was in the air. Why subject children to it? Even with the Depression over, Americans still held down the number of children they produced, fluctuating between 2.3 and 3.1 million. Experts who follow such things say that these were vintage years for people. With fewer births came more room to breathe, compete, grow. The uncertainties of economic instability were there, but the compacted pressure of great numbers of people competing for the same job, home, meal, was not. People born in these years now incorporate the largest number of top executives; they are at the traditional age to wheel and deal and run America's business. Tulane University sociologist Carl L. Harter calls people born in the baby "bust" of the 1930s the nation's first "good times" generation, for today they are in demand to run things and are few in number. Their numbers were further decreased by World War II and Korea. Growing up, they did not experience overcrowded delivery rooms, too-small classrooms, housing shortages or a scarce job market. Because their school classes were smaller, they had a greater chance to learn, to become a member of the debate team or track squad. Their range of activities was unlimited, their chances of becoming well rounded were heightened—and therefore their probability to excel.

Such "good times" began to change between 1947 and 1957. With the World War II over, Americans began to make up for the birth decline in record numbers. The Depression-era anthem of "Happy Days Are Here Again" wafted into the bedroom, and by the time the biggest boom birth year came around in 1957, statistically, each American woman of childbearing age was producing 3.8 children. In that year alone, 4.3 million children were born. A booming postwar economy thrived and it was time to settle down to raise children within the white picket fences of the American Dream. Children born during this euphoria are popularly referred to as "baby-boom babies" today. It is these children who now represent the greatest single bulge in our population. It is these children who would not see "good times" as the Depression children had. They would instead live with the burden of overcrowded classrooms, tight housing, jammed universities. They would go to high schools in split shifts in order to get them all in the door in the first place. They began to compete from the moment they were squeezed into packed maternity rooms. At their high schools there were seven applicants for every opening as a glee club second soprano. They pounded on the doors of the nation's universities in record numbers seeking admission. When they got there, they survived the turbulent Sixties while witnessing the breakdowns of many of their own who could not take the pressure. The competition, the disillusionment with the white picket fence dream was to be a large chunk of their inheritance. Theirs was the generation destined after college to find the competition for jobs so vicious that often the coveted university degree was a key only to driving a taxicab.

Many of these children today hold the levers of power in record numbers. They have a conservatively estimated annual income of $241 billion. That is larger than the Gross National Product of the United Kingdom. When these crowded-times babies opened their mouths a little wider than usual during civil rights demonstrations and Vietnam war protests, the nation listened. It had to, for it has always listened to money. And sheer number. And the promise of potential—if not realized— power. The baby-boom babies, today's 28- to 38-year-olds, brought the median age of the American population down with them when they were born. They began exercising mathematical power from the cradle. And because they constitute one-fifth of the current population of the United States, this generation will take the median age up with it as it grows older. In 1970, the nation's median age was 28, meaning that half the people were older than 28 and the other half younger. By 1981 the median age will be 31; by 2000 it will be 35 and will approach 40 in 2030. In buying power, education, number and, yes, frustration, this is the peak generation. After 1957, American couples took a rest. Children were starving in India and Biafra, and Americans were justifiably spooked by the implications of overpopulation. For the first time in history, inexpensive birth control methods were available—and popularly accepted. The birthrate plummeted from 3.7 children per family in 1958 to 1.8—below the replacement level—in 1976. Some of those responsible for the low birthrate were themselves baby-boom babies. Influenced by ecology, overcrowding and memories of their own competitive child- and adulthoods, they began, consciously or unconsciously, to create another good times generation. It was ironic, for they had never received and would never receive the benefits of the first good times generation.

The tastes of the baby-boom bulge will become the nation's tastes. Their concepts of power, management and mores will set an undisputed tone for the life-styles and professional conduct of future generations. Admittedly, that's a lot of responsibility to plunk down on the shoulders of these still-young adults. But we have offered it and they have accepted it. They have already been seasoned by turbulence, disillusionment and the harsh realities of how American institutions really work. Competition is a given, it seems, for any personal or business activity. The very existence of this generation in record numbers and its struggles to create its own version of the American Dream have infused our culture with the need to achieve things fast—and young.

A few years ago, I had a friend who, by anyone's definition, would be called a young success. He was 25, and the most talked-about columnist for Chicago's most popular newspaper. At an age when most of his journalism contemporaries were writing obituaries for small-town dailies, or scrambling for freelance writing assignments from the Sunday newspaper supplements, my friend had published two books and had a third on the way. He had a nice apartment, a groupie-like following and the jealous jabs of other writers to signal his success. His work seemed glamorous. He was sent by his employer to where the big-breaking news stories were, sometimes to report from foreign countries. He seemed to have it made. Yet every year, on the day the Pulitzer Prizes were announced and his name was not among the all-important winners, my friend would be depressed and mutter dark slogans into his beer. He was "washed up." He would never "make it."

Those who were still aspiring to his level of success couldn't understand this disappointment in the midst of such abundance. To those who were destined by whatever force and circumstance never to make it, his attitude was doubly hard to take, a constant reminder of what they considered their own failure to achieve. To his older colleagues, he was a threat, with precocious intelligence and the added advantage of youth. To those much younger he was, much to his discomfort, endowed with wise and infallible qualities far beyond his years. To his age peers, he was someone to be watched and misunderstood. Perhaps the only people who could sympathize with his Pulitzer blues were other young achievers, who understand that he will probably never be satisfied. And that is one reason why he became successful young.

Yet the "average" achievers in his age group have more in common with him than they realize. For my friend's dissatisfaction, his need to achieve, is the subconscious need of a generation. It is not just, as in the past, the need of a few self-motivated achievers. The fast track must be attained for sheer survival. One need look no further than today's college students to see the effect such competition has already had on succeeding generations. Although fewer in number than the baby boomers, today's college students feel competition perhaps more keenly than did their Sixties predecessors. If the Sixties generation was vocal and maverick, upstart and profane, today's students are just the opposite. Conformity equals good grades equals a good job equals security, and more students are opting for security, unwilling to be as controversial as their Sixties counterparts. As Yale University lecturer William Zinsser writes, the current crop of students "know that the outside world is wary of experimenters, of late starters and temporary losers. . . . Many students come to me in the middle of their sophomore year, afraid of changing the curriculum that they mapped out but no longer think is the one that they want to pursue. 'If I don't make all the right choices now,' one of them said, 'it will be too late.' Too late at 18? Sad words. They are growing up old and set in their ways. They have been told to prepare for one career— preferably one that will reflect well on their parents—and to stick to it and succeed. . . . Today it is more acceptable to change marriage partners than to change careers." We have become a nation of young growing up too fast.

To affect following generations in even this way, and so soon, a generation must have power. The boom babies have always had mathematical power, but only began to realize it in the Sixties. Our conceptions of what is needed to "arrive" have also been altered wherever the boom babies have visited. "I hit California at just the right time," says successful and young Hollywood producer Allan Carr, "right after *The Graduate*. That changed everybody's life. Before that movie, they thought everybody old was brilliant. Afterward, anyone who was young was smart. I rode in on the youth movement." If the character of Benjamin in *The Graduate* expressed the triumphant stand of youth against the shams of an adult society, he also expressed the fears and insecurities of a generation bred in a confusion of values. Beneath the idealism of the youth movement slumbered some serious questions asked by youth itself as to where the momentum was actually heading.

In many cases the momentum was taking the Sixties generation into the business world and into responsible positions rarely held by "young" people. How did that happen? Upon graduation, the boom babies found a large and Vietnam-war-created demand for manufacturing and services. They found a rapidly expanding economy and eager potential employers. Since 1956, employment in industry has increased by 56 percent. These years of go-go growth in the business sector created seemingly limitless possibilities for youth to enter the marketplace. The need to fill new job openings dovetailed with a shortage of Depression-era men who would under normal circumstances be considered at the "right" age for responsibility. "Our economic system grew so fast that there was a real shortage of top management talent," marveled one West Coast executive. "We had no choice but to dig down and grab up young people, many before they were really ready for the responsibility of top management."

In many cases, however, they were ready. The generation that came to young adulthood during the Sixties was in many ways educated for success. It came to expect success, but on its own terms. "See, we were right about the war and we can be right about what's wrong with this society, too," they seemed to trumpet. At the same time companies were creating more growth avenues for themselves and the belligerent young. In 1945 the twenty-five largest United States corporations had an average of six vice-presidential positions each; by 1965 that had shot up to sixteen and ushered in an age of specialization. The rapid development of technology played its role, creating new growth industries such as computers and their care and feeding. Communications reached a level of sophistication undreamed of by previous generations. "Fifty percent of the positions we have today didn't exist even conceptually ten years ago," says Thomas

Theobald, executive vice president of Citibank Corporation. "And that may be a low percentage."

Faced with intense competition, a changing American scene and challenges to the ways business in America had always been conducted, chairmen of the board began to listen for good ideas. If those ideas were sound, it didn't matter so much anymore if the person coming up with them was 48 or 28. And the person with the ideas was not necessarily a White Anglo-Saxon Protestant Male, either. Women began to speak up about something called "equal opportunity." It seemed impractical to waste the talents of 51 percent of the population, and if reasoning and picketing didn't get the idea across, lawsuits did. As a result, the women's movement had far-reaching influence, bringing young, highly educated and competitive women into the job market, as the civil rights movement years before had brought minorities. Affirmative action became a breathing, working fact of corporate life. In many instances, the young woman had an edge over her sisters who had obtained corporate slots before it was "fashionable" for women to do so. "There are many older women who are willing to train and are capable of going on to higher positions within their companies," says New York management consultant Barbara Boyle Sullivan, who helped IBM set up its affirmative action program, "yet the majority of older women, especially those in technical companies, often say, 'If I were younger, I would be willing to spend the time to do what it takes to really make it. But now it's too late for me.' So many companies have turned to the younger woman." If the advantages for young women were slightly greater than those of their older sisters, then they were also slightly greater still than those of their baby-boom brothers. Because of the Vietnam war, many young men were fighting or dying in Southeast Asia. If they weren't in Asia, they were fleeing to Canada or marking time in graduate school to avoid getting involved in what they believed to be an unjust war. This resulted in a shortage of young men to fill some of those expanded positions, and young qualified women stepped in to take charge. The addition of women and minorities brought even more competition into the already intense struggle for position and responsibility.

On paper, at least, sex and race were no longer stumbling blocks to power. The competition that the boom babies had known since infancy began to heat up even more. If the Sixties concepts of change had liberated the young, they also began to liberate the old to compete directly with the young. Suddenly, as a result of changing social consciousness, economic necessity and, perhaps, simple fear of a wave of inexperienced youth running the world, age was no longer a factor in business. Laws were passed, prohibiting employers to discriminate on the basis of age, be it too little or too much. Those men who had been feeling "washed up" at 40 or 50 found they could play on the youth wave and be in demand, too, especially in situations calling for "experience" and "seasoning."

These same situations in which older executives found themselves in demand anew evolved faster than people of any age had imagined. A recession hit. The economy tightened and in the mid-Seventies many companies that had run to the fountain of youthful executives for their talent pulled back, seeking older people for balance. This surprised the quickly employed young who had been given a taste of power in the expanded economy of the late Sixties and early Seventies. The competition that had dogged them reached a boiling point. Women and minorities had expanded the potential executive population. Vietnam veterans began to look for jobs. Industrial expansion was not sufficient to cover the supply of well-educated young. Schoolteachers, lawyers, engineers and those with Ph.D.s found themselves part of a glut as the American socioeconomic scene changed: auto mechanics, appliance repairmen, paramedical specialists and secretaries were now in demand. There were too many chiefs. Suspicious older soothsayers were saying "I told you so." One of the youngest vice presidents in Citibank's history, Thomas Theobald, sees it this way: "Through the Sixties there was an increasing belief that the old fellas had screwed up the world. They brought us World War Two, they couldn't solve the Cold War. But now there's a more cautious view. Maybe it's better to have a sensible and sustainable view than a two-month pop."

The young had been hit with the boomerang of their own youth. Lester B. Korn, president of Korn/Ferry International executive recruiters, views the boomerang in retrospect. "There was a period of time toward the end of the boom in the middle Sixties when there was a real premium for youth," he says. "People said they really needed some bright young people out of the Harvard Business School. And for good or bad that was the way it was. These people moved on to some very significant responsibilities. While I don't believe that that age group made more mistakes than any other age group, their mistakes were very visible. And so when the recession hit—and it was a tremendously deep recession—a premium was placed on experience. The pendulum swung to a point where when before they wouldn't take anyone over forty-five, now they have problems asking someone under fifty."

That prominently held view did not mean that youth was out in the cold entirely. Quite the contrary: companies realized that many times the young were perfect for top positions where risk-taking was essential to the job. Growth industries—computers, semiconductors, leisure activities—couldn't get enough of them. At the same time, companies could dip into the pool of middle-aged executives to temper the risk and supply long-range stability. Ironically, some companies with young executives at the top found themselves eager to hire older executives. One Fortune 500 company that has a 39-year-old chairman has made a practice of hiring managers who are over the age of 45 to provide experienced viewpoints for planning and development in new product areas. Business, then, has been presented with the option of growing its own or bringing in experienced people, a situation that has been misinterpreted by some to mean that only middle-aged executives have an edge in today's market. They don't—they have just made the competition even tougher. "When things are tough you don't bring in people to be eventual vice presidents," says G. William Moore, president of the National Employment Service of Raleigh, North Carolina. "You look for experience. You're not building character for the future. You're not an educational institution." The simple economic fact that for every dollar a company spends in salary for the training of a young executive it must also factor in three to four additional dollars in investment costs began to hit where it hurt, on the bottom line. Knowing that it could expect to pay $45,000 to $60,000 for a $15,000 trainee, and that its investment would not pay dividends for from two to five years down the road, the American company began to be cautious about its investments in young candidates. It could afford to be selective in hiring the young risk-taker with energy and academic degrees to spare.

Once again competition bashed the baby boomers over the head. In response, many felt an edge could be obtained via a graduate degree. While business pulled back, educational institutions were turning out graduates in record numbers. Young lawyers, executives, teachers, engineers became plentiful. Colleges and universities handed out 123,000 master's degrees in education each year—to accommodate schools that had overbuilt and overstaffed in anticipation of the wave of post-baby-boom children that never came.

This degree overload in the face of a significant population decrease has created a glutted teaching market. But the overwhelming pressure just to get a job in one's chosen profession is not the exclusive preserve of education. In the business sector it is no better. While the economy is just beginning to recover from the recession that followed three decades of expansion after World War II, industrial capacity is barely 70 percent realized. The rapid business promotion rate of the Sixties is no more, but still the flood of MBAs continues. In 1964 fifteen colleges handed out 6,000 MBAs; in 1977 a total of 550 schools handed out 35,000 advanced business degrees. For every MBA student accepted at Stanford's business school in 1977, fifteen were rejected. Ten years ago, the ratio was one acceptance to six rejections. This state of affairs, observers say, will lead to a bust in business education in the 1980s as the number of available jobs remains at today's constricted levels, or even declines.

===

*Books in Print* currently lists two hundred seventy books with "Success" prominent in their title. "Success under 35," reads the headline on a full-page New York *Times* ad for *Glamour* magazine. "How ten *Glamour* readers made it." In that magazine's annual "success choices" selection of the ten outstanding career women in the United States, many featured women have accomplished in their twenties what most of us take a lifetime to achieve. To read the feats of a 23-year-old self-made woman millionairess, or a 25-year-old woman who is making $60,000 as an executive vice president of a marketing firm, is enough to drive the average achiever under the table in despair. If said achiever is 26, the despair plunges to an all-time low. Why? Because success under 35 has become not just the rare and sanctified province of those special few who are endowed with luck, smarts, and drive, but an absolute necessity for the protest generation so blessed with education and opportunity. Using a landmark study on the boom generation conducted by Daniel Yankelovich, *Playboy* magazine runs an expensive series of full-page ads in the New York *Times*. The series praises the intensity of the Sixties generation and chronicles its vast spending habits. "Good news for American Business: Today's young men are getting richer, quicker," it heralds, calling the current under-35s "the new materialists."

Sure, they burned draft cards and tore up the campus and smoked funny cigarettes and never cut their hair and made us despair . . . but now? Ah, now "they haven't lost one iota of that intensity. They've just totally redirected it. They've traded the SDS for IBM and GM . . ." And apparent riches. Their average income is $16,000, but the ads feature real-life young men who make far, far more. The ads are illustrated with pictures of young executives playing tennis, leaning on expensive small foreign sports cars, wearing fur coats. They look successful, rich. Young.

To be successful young is the new American ideal, ironically at a time when our population base is getting older. The reminders that we must make it young, that it's too late if we wait for even a moment, are everywhere. Consciously or not, we compare ourselves to the young men and women in the ads, in the news, on the television. Am I making $16,000 at age 21? If I am 23 now, could I buy a tennis racket like his by next year on my salary? If so, could I afford the tennis court to use it on? If I am 34 and a junior executive still, does that mean something is somehow wrong with me? America has always been impressed with those who charge to the front early. But the fast track is no longer just for those who eagerly and voluntarily test its cinders with eyes wide open and muscles ready. Candle-makers and macramé-threading organic gardeners excepted, the rest of our youth have been forced onto that track, like it or not, by sheer momentum and peer pressure. Not only are their eyes not quite open, but many of them haven't had the chance to warm up properly.

The fast track has created tremendous pressure on those within and without the baby-boom bulge. The swift ones who are on it, and those who have been left at the post, are in the middle of a powerful societal change which is at the same time constructive and perilous. "An article of faith in management since 1917 is that your first rule should be to recruit all the good people you can and then worry later about what's going to happen to them," says Citibank's Theobald. But worry about the effects of forced fast trackery we must. In a *Time* magazine forum on leadership, published in 1976, former Federal Trade Commission Chairman Lewis A. Engman, now a Washington attorney, listed the most dominant element constraining the emergence of leadership in America as fear: "Fear of making mistakes, fear of taking risks, fear of letting the press look over our shoulder, fear of not being successful."

One man who has seen these problems coming is Peter H. Engel, himself an industry "quick study" in his rise to the presidency of Helena Rubinstein. Engel, author of *The Over-achievers*, a book on driven executives, notes that the fewer-in-number Depression babies are themselves "Reaching power at a relatively younger age. And they will hold on to that power. If you reach power by age 40, there's nothing to suggest that you're going to give it up in the normal ten-year span. These people will have an even higher amount of power because they have had twenty years to create it." How will this situation affect the young adults of the Sixties, who have already had a heady dose of power at a young age? "Today you have twice as many people per job—men and women. And when the lines of students appear at the recruiters door, the young person who gets the job cannot by any means be sure that by doing a decent job and keeping her nose clean, she's going to get a promotion. So she has to, by the nature of the animal, do something spectacular. She has to do something in order to stand out in the crowd, and that means there is a higher need for dynamic achievement. In order to get a promotion you have to dramatize yourself and your achievement. Only then can you afford to risk failure."

In a 1977 research paper on managers and promotion, published by the Columbia University Graduate School of Business, the need for superior performance from the outset in today's business world is underscored. "Tightening economic and competitive conditions, as well as technological progress, will make it increasingly difficult for organizations to carry individuals whose potential is low or whose performance is less than outstanding, particularly in view of the need to provide opportunities and challenges for other aspiring managers," it says in part. No wonder today's college students keep their mouths shut and worry. Already, according to Eugene Jennings, a management specialist at Michigan State University, the theories of the Columbia study have come to pass. In his book *The Mobile Manager*, Jennings notes:

> Today the men at the top are products of compressed experience, the stresses of which not everyone was able to stand. In fact, the mobile manager has left behind a large number of casualties. . . . The mobile manager has exploded the myth that the ulcer level exists at the corporate zenith. The fact is that the incident of psychosomatic illness is significantly higher among members of the passed-over generation, as well as the premature death rate due to heart attack and suicide. . . . For many, stress without success has become unbearable during this period of high mobility.

Today's risk-taking adult young have the same fear of failure as those adults whose business practices they criticized when they were college students. Perhaps their fear is even greater. Ironic—was the vocal generation of the Sixties ever supposed to know the meaning of the word "failure"? They were crowded, yes, but also endowed with the best education, most sophisticated dissemination of information, than any group in our history. They had won major successes as a group even before entering the marketplace. Yes, we stopped a war. Yes, we shook the bedrock of American culture. Yes, we made you question. Yes, we made our culture and tasted yours. The unthinkable thought of youth—that one could not do absolutely everything, know everything, that one could fail—is deeply rooted in this generation. And it is rooted in the midst of more success gained in a shorter period of time than any other generation has experienced.

"What we have created here is an environment in which the rules are developing as fast as the game is played," says Jennings, who for twenty years has kept close and scholarly watch on the executives who run America's corporations, chronicling the changes that affect them:

> It's a terribly competitive world in which we have fantastic constraints placed upon corporations. It's harder and harder to make a buck. We have inside the corporation all kinds of action programs that we have to sponsor. Give the blacks a chance. Give women a chance. I don't know of one corporation that doesn't believe that is going to keep capitalism alive. The fight is over, and it wasn't much of a fight. The real fight now is here in the middle, with all these young constituting a critical mass. We have a bunch of thirty-year-olds near the middle of the apex here that sort of moved en masse into the corporation in the Sixties and early Seventies. And they're sitting there.

The woes of Jennings' "critical mass" are not confined to business: in law firms, university classrooms, newspaper city rooms, large publishing houses, television studios and political campaign headquarters the problem exists on the same scale.

Given this fight in the middle, this economy, this competition, such swings of the social and economic pendulum, who became the most successful of the successful "bad times" generation? Each age group has within its ranks that special 8 or so percent who made it on their own, made it to places even their high-flying, affluent and fast-track peers could not have dared to reach in twice as much time. We shall not deal with mathematical or scientific geniuses, child prodigies who compose symphonies in the cradle or teenage singers/movie stars/dancers /track stars. All these people have certain gifts that take them out of the mainstream, special talents that deserve other books.

We will deal instead with those people with whom we probably went to school, who, seen on the street, might very well not strike us as rich or successful at first glance. We shall meet the self-motivated who did not inherit daddy's company but instead made their own way to the top in record time, in these peculiar times that combine opportunity and intense competition. We shall meet those who exemplify some very old-fashioned pioneer values tempered with some very new ideas of consciousness, self-confidence and self-worth. We shall meet those who set the pace.

Those who have emerged as superachievers are perhaps the most prepared, ambitious, personally and professionally successful group of people this nation has ever seen. It is through them and a study of their ambitions, talents and influence that we can begin to understand the new notion of success in America and the ways its definition has changed in the wake of turbulent political and social times. It is through these bad times/good times youth that we can see what a philosophical and practical impact their generation has had, is having and will have on our lives. It is through them we can see the future.

Who becomes successful while young these days? How did they get there so quickly when equally talented, educated and intelligent—not to mention equally competitive and ambitious— peers are still achieving what their "traditional" age level says they should achieve? How, in the midst of the most competitive generation America has ever produced, did they make it? How have they altered the concept of "making it"? What makes these new young lions different? What are the threads that tie them to the fabric of values that created our nation and extend to its future?

Perhaps the most important thing we can learn from an examination of young success is the framework to examine our own motivations by our own individual sense of competitiveness, our own needs and desires to be personally and professionally happy. The answers are there, in part. They are already in our young. And while these successful young do not have all the answers we had hoped they would, they have a start. There is something very different about them and their generation. The things that made them special provide a framework for coping in today's world. Surprisingly, we do have many things in common with them. And they have many things in common with each of us.

# 2 ▤ The Need to Achieve: First Step to Power

IT SEEMS THAT for every group of humans there is a study. We have dissected the personalities of disturbed children, Nobel Prize winners, gifted children, geniuses and convicts. There have been sociological studies on tycoons and assembly-line workers. Minority children, managerial women, divorced men, child prodigies, saints and psychopathic killers have all had their day under the methodological microscope. But there exists not one study about why people become successful young, and how we can predict who among us is destined to charge ahead while the rest chart an average course.

Scholarly tomes and quick "pop" studies on successful people list various qualities that such people have, but do little to tell us how these factors have contributed to the individual's success. What do such factors mean beyond their surface definitions and how can we apply what we have read? Psychological and business journals regularly publish de rigueur essays, polls and ministudies on leadership, success, the entrepreneurial and executive personality and corporate presidents. Such articles usually include a "Top 40" listing of qualities needed for the job. One study says originality, popularity, sociability, judgment, aggressiveness, the desire to excel, humor, cooperativeness, liveliness and athletic ability are factors essential to successful leadership. Another gives the following recipe for success: intelligence, verbalization skills, integrity, self-acceptance, leadership (defined as the ability to get things done), adaptability, desire to achieve, determination, persistence, commitment and such "accidental" factors as good health and good luck. Good grief—one study of successful men and women merely lists talent, luck and persistence. Another heralds hard work, period.

To another extreme, take a March, 1977, Institutional Investor psychological profile of successful money managers. This poll took such general concepts as "luck" and "determination" and sought to break them down into more manageable and recognizable factors. Thus, instead of asking money managers if they liked being competitive, the magazine asked them if they wanted to be secret service men or auto racers or foreign correspondents, and compared their answers to mainstream American responses. Instead of asking them if they liked playing hard, the magazine compared their interests in more translatable terms: money managers, it was found, like formal dress affairs, playing the piano and bridge better than did the average man, but were less likely to want to "pursue bandits in a sheriff's posse" and "adjust a carburetor" than John Q. Public would. Such a study could come in handy if one had a broken carburetor and ran into a money manager on the highway, but for predicting where their success came from, it had its weak moments. It was valuable in pinpointing personality types via more specific criteria, but the origins were left unexplored. Elsewhere, a more traditional study tells us that successful people set goals, make lists and believe in the American Dream. Another tells us that the ability to seize and recognize opportunity is important, that creativity, self-reliance, the willingness to accept responsibility are keys to success. The sea of speculation, however ill- or well-defined, is vast.

"But I set goals," many of us could argue. "I am pretty smart and certainly grab at opportunity when I see it. My friends tell me I'm creative and my girlfriend/boyfriend tells me I'm persistent. So why am I not successful at a young age? What do these hotshots have that I don't have, anyway?" Granted, each of us has elements of all the success and leadership factors listed in studies, and many of us have those extra qualities that are shared by those who make it to the top and make it young. The problem comes in recognizing these extras and seeing how they function, understanding where these qualities come from in the first place and how we can develop and apply them. Through the young successes of today we can see where achievement begins and how those faceless attributes have come alive. And perhaps we can recognize the important basics ourselves, and act accordingly.

Historian Richard Huber says that the American definition of success lies in not just being rich and famous, but the attainment of such wealth and fame. "You had to know where a man began in order to judge how far he's come," Huber says, and he is right. It is not the story of the wealthy prep school scion who rises to head his father's corporation that we as a nation relish. It is instead the against-all-odds climb of a tattered newsboy (supporting, ideally, a widowed mother and invalid grandfather, while at the same time working his way through night school) to become ruler of a vast publishing empire. How did he get there? is what we want to know. Now that's a story—if he can get there, maybe we can, too. Ralph Waldo Emerson once noted that "the world belongs to the energetic." Perhaps it does. But surely energy alone does not separate the average man or woman and the superachiever. Energy merely enables the

many facets of their personalities to emerge. Energy is a catalyst
for the chemistry of success. Such chemistry and its effect to
produce early bloomers has not been studied before.

Like the profiles of tycoons and gifted children, the profiles
of young achievers are a complex combination of factors.
Home and social environment, family pressure and practices,
economic and ethnic variables must all be considered. But at the
top of the list for achievers, in general, and young superachievers
in particular, is one all-important quality that separates the doers
from the drifters—*the need to achieve.* Such people *must*
achieve, and they are driven by an intense need to be Somebody.
Drive is the most important of the myriad qualities needed to
achieve. Drive is that peculiar hunger to extend oneself, to test
oneself constantly, to excel. Thus, drive is the starting point.
"Keeping up one's drive is comparable with keeping vigilance on
the security of one's country," writes Nicolas Darvas in *The
Anatomy of Success.* "The greatest danger facing the individual
—and one which seems to cause the largest number of dropouts
in the success game—is the temptation to relax this drive."

The temptation, for the majority of the population, comes
at an early age. In college and shortly after, career patterns are
formed. Most people settle. Their drive plateaus, and is maintained at a noncompetitive level or pitch, for whatever reason.
They accept their place in the scheme of things, and go no
further than the average. Therefore, the game of young achievement is pretty well lost at the start, regardless of how much
talent, intelligence and general savvy one might have. For without the drive to go a bit further, the individual stays put.

Those who become young successes don't stay put—not
even for the amount of time it takes to enjoy what success they
have earned at the moment. Something drives them to achieve
even more. Every one of the young successes interviewed mentioned drive as the key factor in their lives. Some of them understood from where their individual motivation comes. Others

knew such burning ambition existed, but did not know, or did not care to find out, the sources that contributed to the need inside them. Where does this hunger come from? All of us have it, to one degree or another. To cultivate it, to understand it, is the beginning of the ability to use it, and the start of the road to achievement.

Yet where such drive comes from is not easily deciphered. One explanation of this need to achieve as seen through those who possess it comes from William James. In *The Varieties of Religious Experience*, he defines two basic personality types. People who are "once-born" are the accepters, those who tend to go along with the status quo and indeed constitute the status quo. Those once-born, James says, are those whose lives have been harmonious, for the most part. The feeling of contentment that is theirs comes from a feeling of being in tune with their environment and the people who populate it. Once-borns could be said to be those who belong—perhaps the envied high school football captain, class president or cheerleader. They are the students who seemed to have it made, those who were not "pushy" in our adolescent definition. A once-born could be the peacemaker, the hail fellow well met. Once out of school the once-born is likely to become a manager whose satisfaction comes from being part of a team effort. In such an effort, the status quo is maintained and change, when it occurs, is harmonious and smooth.

A once-born, while serving as the backbone of society and making unquestionably valuable contributions to it, does not rock the boat. Probably 80 percent of the population could fall into this average achiever category, according to management consultants, personnel officers and others who see the effects of drive and its ebb and flow on American life. That is not to say that 80 percent of the population does not want to get ahead. Nor does that imply the bulk of the population has had an easy life with few traumas and hardships. For the purposes of studying young overachievers, the plethora of once-born represents the reality that, at base, most people wish to be led rather than take on the strains, the responsibilities and difficult decisions of leadership. Most people are content to be useful and productive members of a team, creating no waves and enjoying the fruits of cooperative mainstream efforts. Once-borns are regulators, bureaucrats. They are the canvas.

The paint, the splash of color, is the twice-born, James's second personality type. The twice-born are not managers, but instead are the leaders, who revel in smashing icons and being different. The lives of the twice-borns are spent in a kind of struggle to attain that harmony the once-borns seem to enjoy, perhaps to play catch-up to the once-borns who seem to have everything together. An absence of a parent, excessive parental pressure, the presence of family difference or difficulty—any number of external and internal factors can account for the separateness a twice-born feels. In high school, America's coming-of-age battleground, the twice-borns could be classified as the "outies," those who were somehow not part of the group. This very difference often makes twice-borns succeed in life. Sometimes they succeed spectacularly and early. Why? A feeling of separateness can often supply a vision of leadership in the future, and can be a powerful shaping force. Call it the "outside looking in" syndrome if you will—perhaps a child has a difficult home life and is not accepted by his/her family or peers; perhaps a child has a good home life with much educational input and is more advanced than his/her peers—whether the root be a good or bad situation, the result is often the same. The result could be manifest in an "I'll show you" attitude, a defiance born of separateness. Or it could take shape as a quiet despair at not being able to be part of the mainstream. The twice-born will often possess intense drive, born of difference.

"In order to be successful, one has to be different. A different style of doing things, perhaps. A different approach to business problems. A different method of promotion," Darvas writes. Such difference in the twice-borns is intensified in school. Although ideally children in our educational system are taught to be individuals, to realize their potential as such, those who in any way deviate from the norm are punished, by peers or teachers—or both. Whatever the source of individuality, a twice-born is apt to turn separateness inward, in some cases creating a world of fantasy. In some cases, the desire for revenge is uppermost in the mind. In some cases the twice-born will attempt to beat the mainstream at its own game. Whether the reason be to reconcile family problems or avenge a lack of peer or adult acceptance doesn't matter.

What does matter is the modus operandi. If the twice-born belongs to an institution, it will not be as your average member, content to go along with the crowd. A twice-born will use groups and yet not be a part of them. Institutions, schools, job categories, social sets and other trappings do not in themselves make up the identity of the twice-born. The identity comes instead from within, from the complicated inner struggles that have led to the feeling of being different. This feeling provides the fuel for the drive. Twice-borns use the society's institutions to gain certain satisfactions, to accomplish certain things. But in the end for them it is the conquering of the self that produces the most lasting psychological and social change. A self-reliance emerges, an independence is born of isolation. Whatever the roots of the separateness, an astute twice-born will take them and plant them, nourish and use them to become wiser still. If this happens, a twice-born becomes a leader, with an edge the once-born cannot have. If the twice-born is very sharp, has learned the lessons well and is able to take risks to achieve what is important to him or her, that twice-born can become a young success. The makings are already there.

The need to achieve and its consequent success could also be explained by difference in personality type. Recently it has been popular to cast people as either "Type A" or "Type B" personalities. This measure has been primarily used to see if doctors can predict what factors would make a person prone to heart attacks, nervous breakdowns, ulcers and presumably, early death. The Type A personality is achievement-oriented, is hard on oneself, looks for goals and honors and, on balance, is highly competitive. Type A's work hard and fast to succeed. Type B's, on the other hand, are more easygoing, less likely to bring work home, more relaxed in general. Type B is less likely to receive academic honors than is Type A, although in many cases the Type B is equally intelligent. Type B's could be classified as once-borns; Type A's, twice borns.

There are other viable measures that can be applied to the examination of young success. In their book *Entrepreneurship and the Corporation*, William Copulsky and Herbert McNulty examine what constitutes the personality of the entrepreneur, the self-made American business success. Their measures stand side by side with the theories of those who classify people by personality type. Taken all together, the traits studied can provide a blueprint for mapping ambition. Copulsky and McNulty see the entrepreneur as separate from the mainstream, set off by a sense of his difference. The entrepreneur possesses a high energy level, restlessness, a willingness to work hard and take risks, a desire to escape from insecurity. Many other studies—of Fortune 500 presidents, successful businessmen or political leaders—could apply to the study of young success. Even the Institutional Investor Survey of money managers' affection for pianos and hostility toward carburetors and sheriff's posses reveals a valuable piece of the mosaic. There is room for a profusion of traits and factors, for motivation and achievement are complex and touchy areas of study.

Yet the key question in the success game is whether young leaders, or young successes, are born or made. Can you educate for early success, or is achievement somehow preordained and unalterable? No examination of the need to achieve can be complete without an explanation of those theories that apply to motivation. For instance, what would Sigmund Freud say about a hard-driving young success? Freud sees motivation as coming from drives created deep within the individual's unconscious. The parent–child relationship is important here. In Freud's view, the struggle for power between parent and child is pivotal from birth, and such a struggle never ends. In psychoanalytical schools, intense drive often comes from irrational and antisocial places, hidden in the furrows of the unconscious. Highly self-motivated people can't be followers because they resent a powerful authority over them, with the resentment stemming from unresolved fears of the father figure. Freud might not be a welcome guest at a young successes convention, for he would probably put such highly achievement-oriented folk on an unappetizing scale somewhere between neurotic and psychotic.

A cheerier view in the psychoanalytical school is that of psychiatrist Eric Berne. Berne sees our twice-borns, entrepreneurs or Type A's, as following behavior patterns ("scripts") that have been written by their families since birth. If a child is told stories of success, either from parents who are themselves successful, or parents who wish they were, such children are more likely to be achievement-oriented.

Behavioral psychologists see drive as coming from a different source. Behaviorists say that motivation comes from external influences rather than the cobwebs of the mind. Though this might at first glance seem to be a kinder school to the young success type, such is not entirely the case. The strongly motivated in this school are viewed as not being quite representative of normal, mainstream behavior. In many respects, of course, achievers are not. Comparing the achievements and modus operandi of a young success with that of the average achiever population, these driven are in a separate—and small—group. In the behavioral view, motivation is born when one is different from the norm. Perhaps one is a member of a minority, or has family traditions and practices different from the mainstream. Perhaps the family is poor, or less loving, or extremely loving. Such a feeling of separateness in the home makes highly motivated people strike out on their own and begin an energetic quest for independence. Such people have started out as being different in some way, and in one sense would have nothing to lose by being far different still. They are not afraid to take risks. They can see things from another viewpoint and won't be held back with verbal roadblocks like: "That's not the way it's done." Behaviorists say that a high achiever reacts to the stimuli around him—ethnic taunts, lack of compassion by peers or a feeling of superiority over peers—by being more separate, more distinct. In the end, the independence they crave is accomplished by achieving.

Enter psychologist Abraham Maslow and his humanistic school. This is perhaps the most encouraging philosophy to the highly motivated who are tired of being branded neurotic, disturbed and somehow not quite normal by other theories. Under Maslow's roof, the highly achievement-oriented individual is so because he or she actually likes being a doer, enjoys work and is rewarded by the fruits of his or her labors. A happy and well-adjusted superachiever is Maslow's ideal of the fulfillment of human potential. Such an individual sits at the top of Maslow's hierarchy of needs, a ladder of wants and desires that is Maslow's measure of development. The lowest rung in the hierarchy comprises basic needs—food, clothing and shelter. These must be satisfied before an individual can begin to explore the less tangible realms of potential. Once clothed, housed and fed, the individual's next step on the ladder is to stabilize his environment, to keep it safe and secure. After that, the individual turns to a third level—social needs, reaching out to others, making and keeping friends, sharing resources. A sense of belonging begins here. On the fourth rung, the ego begins to take over and the individual needs not only to have friends but to be recognized by them. Self-confidence is important at this stage. But the need to be important is saved for the last step, that of self-fulfillment. This happens only when an individual grows and develops through the other stages, and at this fifth level we find the young successes. While their peers may have achieved security, shelter, friends and some ego, the young success type goes one step further to self-actualization. The perceptive superachiever recognizes that the first four steps in Maslow's hierarchy arise from a lack of something, but the final step comes from the need to add, to supplement. It embodies an eager, spontaneous and creative desire to realize the full potential of the individual.

Lest all those who champion the young success type be tempted to lionize Maslow, a word of caution: neither Maslow, nor Freud, nor James, nor, in fact, any one school of thought can fully and adequately explain where drive comes from. That is an encouraging statement for those who are young successes, for they abhor being neatly categorized, accurately dissected. They defy slots and simplistic explanations. The explanation of drive lies within the individual—some young successes interviewed could happily snuggle up with Freud, others with Maslow, and still others with the behaviorists or William James. But they possess, as a breed, many characteristics that cut across age, social, class and ethnic barriers, motivations whose roots lie in all schools of thought.

In a series of in-depth interviews with many who personify the young success story in America, it is easy to see, in some of them, a striving for power and resentment of authority. In others, there is a clear cultural estrangement, an alienation that became a source of great strength, as the behavioral school proposes. For others still, motivation comes from sheer joy in doing work that is rewarding and—a word not often heard these days —simply fun. Motivation emerges from many sources. Each of us has to some degree the drive and abilities found in young success types. The trick is how to channel these characteristics, how best to nurture them. But the biggest feat is to recognize them in the first place. How do the young successes make it?

━━

It is popular for professors and students of the success ethic to view men and women who have achieved and credit the result to the marvels of hitching planning to hard work. In school we are taught to have goals, to think always of the future, to make a three- or five- or even ten-year plan for our aspirations. We are told that leadership qualities are born of such planning. We are told that extracurricular activities will make us "well-rounded" individuals ripe for achievement. In school, we look enviously at those students who have good grades, those who belong to the student council, glee club and football or cheerleader squad. We think that these blessed few are destined for—indeed assured—of success. It seems these people plan for the future. They are tidy, organized. But not everybody knows from the age of ten if the life of a bank president is for him or her. There are no five-year plans for success for many of us. The ever-present (and sometimes dreaded) adult question "What do you want to be when you grow up?" is not always easily answered, or the answer changes on a regular basis. What to do when all the textbooks seem to say that success comes to those who work toward a set goal, that true success was never achieved by mere luck?

While it is true that luck alone and fifty cents will get you a subway ride and little else, the textbooks in part are quite wrong. Success in general—and young success in particular— does not always come to those who sang in the glee club, had straight white teeth and planned each intense day with the urgency of Eisenhower mapping out the Normandy invasion. Success can come not only to those who so plan and work, but also to those who seemingly stumbled on opportunity and grabbed it. Perhaps these people were in the right place at the right time, helped or surrounded by the right people. And perhaps, if you asked them what they wanted to be when they grew up, they *still* couldn't tell you. But that doesn't make them any less successful. Half of those successes interviewed were achievers all along. They had gobbled up extracurricular activities, scholastic and community honors like popcorn. They had carefully planned and worked toward set goals. But the other half "fell" into success, were not achievers in school, did not make the honor society and hadn't the least idea what they wanted to do in life. Things for these people seemed to just happen and one day—voilà!—success.

If one can't predict future success solely on the basis of planning and organization, what about birth order? There have been many studies on the importance of being a first-born, or an only child. Such children, it is said, are more likely to be independent, self-assured and, perhaps, successful. Their personalities are stronger, and so are their leadership qualities. The attention an only child receives from adults is important—there is no competition for love. The expectations of the parents are intensely placed in such a child. Having such an adult home environment also contributes to greater self-reliance and, ideally, a good adjustment to the adult world outside the home. First-borns also get the attention of their parents. They too are expected to achieve, to set an example for their siblings. While it is true that many of the young successes interviewed were indeed first-borns or "onlys," it is also true that just as many were the youngest of four, the middle of three, the seventh of seven or the second of five. True to the young-success trait of avoiding categorization as much as possible, each of them tried to explain at least part of their drive in terms of individual birth order.

"Well, I was the first child and of course I was expected to achieve," one man would say, while another would explain, "I was the middle of three and of course I had to achieve to make up for not being the oldest (favored) or youngest (babied)." "I'm an only and you know what they say about onlys," one woman would confide, as another would say the same thing about being the fourth-born in a family of five boys. Each young success justified birth order as an important part of motivation —and each birth order was different from the next.

Planning and birth order, then, are not always accurate predictors of young success. What about intelligence? Surely those who are superachievers are those whose grades were the best, whose perceptions were the most admired, whose IQs were right up there with those of the Science Club presidents. An excess of smarts would transcend birth order, a five-year plan and a letter sweater with oak-leaf clusters. Not so. Many of the young successes are good examples of academic excellence, of course. Many did belong to the honor society, were recognized for their intelligence (which, as we shall see later, in some cases was cause for an estrangement from peers) and did get good grades. But just as many, perhaps more than half, were not academic whiz kids. Some barely squeaked by in high school or college. Some received straight C's and D's in high school, then went on to get straight A's in college. Others reversed that pattern. Some did not finish college at all. And many were academically simply average.

The question of education and its value in preparing students for later life is a thorny one. No one can deny that education is an important and necessary credential to enter the working world. To have the skills needed to function in society, to be able to read, reason, do mathematical problems, is a given. But in a country where the level of education compared to the rest of the world is relatively high, the issue becomes a matter of how education can be effectively used. Is it enough to be able to diagram a sentence, take a test, measure up to a conventional academic standard? Or is that just the beginning? Should our educational institutions be doing something more?

That debate continues. Its relationship to the development of leadership skills, to becoming successful in later life, is an important one, and there is an emerging body of thought that says something more must be added if we are to truly create and nourish leaders as we say we do. The findings of one study lending support to this point of view were revealed in June, 1977. Douglas Heath, a professor of psychology at Haverford College, had been studying sixty-eight male graduates of a small liberal arts college for fifteen years. The graduates had all been honor students. Was there a link between their academic success and achievement later on in life? The study found that there was not; that, based on the sample, good grades and academic honors do not necessarily correspond with personal maturity and competence. The honor students studied were "less effective" as adults than their classmates who received less academic success. Relationships with their wives, for instance, were not so close or so warm as those in the nonhonor group. As adults, the academic whizzes were found to be aloof and tense with business associates, and said to have an "inaccurate understanding" of themselves in general.

The study found that success was most closely linked, not with grades, but with such nonacademic factors as moral values, character development and an empathetic understanding of and relation to others. Such findings help to reassure those of us who received C's and feel reasonably well adjusted. While they are not meant as an absolute, they do show that standard measures of intelligence do not necessarily predict how successful a person will be. Indeed, the study calls academic measures "absolute failures to predict a variety of adult competencies." If this study is any indication, those institutions stressing only academic excellence would do well to consider nonacademic factors to better prepare their students for lives as competent and fulfilled adults.

If intelligence, birth order and careful All American goal-tending are not in and of themselves indicators of early success, what factors are? What do those careful career planners with high/low grades, and those lucky, unorganized young successes with high/low grades, have in common with their first-born/only/last-born/middle sibling counterparts at the top of the young superachiever ladder? As we will see in the next chapter, the answer is . . . plenty. But before finding such personal common denominators, it might be intriguing to examine what tools we do have with which to predict who will be an early success. Can we forecast who will make it and who won't? David Winter, associate professor of psychology at Wesleyan University, thinks we can. Winter and his associates—Harvard psychology professor David C. McClelland and Boston University assistant psychology professor Abigail Stewart—completed a fifteen-year study in late 1977, a study that for the first time attempted to corral those traits that lead to early success. It also attempted to formulate a scientific set of success predictors.

The researchers studied one hundred members of the class of 1964 at "Ivy College," a pseudonymous all-male university in the northeast. Their first job was to formulate working definitions of what success is. Incorporating objective and subjective measures, they came up with these six "areas" to measure success:

> 1. Career Fulfillment: A subject could be termed successful if he rates himself as happy and satisfied with his job. If he has an interesting job, achieves some form of recognition, feels good about his life and his vocation, it is one measure of achievement.
> 2. Income: The subject does not have to necessarily be rich. In the case of a teacher, the level of professor is a mark of success. For a lawyer, it could be a prestigious law firm; for a banker, a partnership.

3. Measures of Early Success: In this category, a subject is seen to achieve faster. He has laid the foundation in an obvious way. Perhaps he gets a graduate degree or is a member of a well-connected social set.

4. Organizational Power: A subject who is successful might have membership in many outside organizations, and may hold offices in same. He may be politically active. He makes full use of his skills, on the job and outside it, and his job allows him to be satisfied. If the man has a wife who holds a traditional "male" job, this is a big plus.

5. Unreasonable Time Demands: This negative category is also a measure of success. A successful man is also one who is hassled and overwhelmed. Does he work too hard? Does his job take up too much time? Is the job prestigious, but perhaps not pleasant?

6. Professional Category: Is the subject in a field that lets him grow? Does he have good social relationships at work? Does the bureaucracy of his profession allow him the freedom to pursue self-fulfillment? Is his job a prestigious one?

Among the variables the researchers took into account in predicting these six success categories were two measures of social background (IQ and social class), four measures from the Thematic Aperception Test (TAT) that the group took in 1964 as freshmen at the college; cumulative college grades and three measures of the subject's current family situation. Using these variables, what characteristics will predict any or several of the six success measurement categories? The study blew apart some old myths and reinforced others. Winter and his associates arrived at five key predictors of success.

First, they found controlled interest in power will predict having that power fifteen years later. If a person wants to have an impact on people and is recognized as such, this can predict success, especially Organizational Power (factor four). The researchers call this first category Leadership/Motive.

Second, in a category dubbed Erickson/Freud, the study says using the theories of emotional maturity formulated by Erik Erickson and Sigmund Freud, the more mature the subject is as a college freshman:

a. the more satisfied he will be fifteen years later
b. the more organizational power he will have
c. the more overwhelmed by his work he will be
d. the less likely he will be to work in a strict bureaucracy
e. the more income he will have

In short, five out of the six success categories are predicted. If one fits these theories of maturity the more likely it is that he will be happy in his work.

Third, the matter of Scholastic Aptitude Test (SAT) scores. Such scores, the researchers found, were absolutely unrelated to career fulfillment and rapid success. There was a slight correlation between high SATs and the feeling of Being Overwhelmed. SAT scores were negatively related to Organizational Power. They had a slight relationship to High Income and did not predict either rapid success or happiness.

Fourth, Social Class. If the subject was in the upper middle to upper class he was more apt to be unsatisfied. High social class had a negative correlation to Organizational Power and Being Overwhelmed.

Fifth, Senior College Grades. Having high grades in one's last year in college positively—and significantly—predict early success. But such grades negatively predict Career Fulfillment.

One interesting aspect of the study is the discovery that the wife's career level is an extremely powerful predictor of career fulfillment. The more difficult his wife's career, the more satisfied the subject was with his own career. A career fulfilling and challenging to his wife is associated with Organizational Power, High Income and the feeling of Being Overwhelmed. It is a most vivid predictor. For this group of men, being married and getting good grades in college were the two important forerunners of success.

Predicting success is a thorny—and new—business. Predicting early success is doubly so. The Winters study is the first longitudinal look at the subject. Yet it is only a part of a larger tome exploring the effects of college. More specific research is needed to further define and predict the slippery breed who rise to the top fast, but this particular study has given powerful guidelines.

The routes to the top for young successes can be straight superhighways leading toward a mountain or a series of rutted, unmarked country roads lacking direction and sprinkled with dead ends. Motivation alone, planning alone, goal-setting alone, intelligence alone—all do not in and of themselves make an achiever an achiever. It is only when a few or many of these traits are combined—much like combining separate parts of an automobile engine—that an achiever evolves. The engine that makes each of us go has many of the same parts as that which makes a young success go. We each have ambition, energy, desire for wealth, the ability to see and grasp opportunity, the ability to learn and other "success" qualities to a greater or lesser degree. But the difference emerges in how we combine and use those qualities. What makes up that special oomph, that STP of the soul, that something extra that enables some of us to achieve quickly? The answer is complex, and lies just as much with an individual's own chemistry as it does with ancient or contemporary explanations of what makes us run. In the next chapter we'll examine that chemistry, and see how it has worked for others. We'll also see how that chemistry we possess could work for us.

# 3 ≣ Planning or Luck?
# The Roots of Success

THOSE WHO HAVE made it to the top young these days are likely to be loners, pure and simple. It is a misconception that all of the people who make it young are the most popular in school. They are not likely to be the most athletic or accepted. The term "loner" can have both positive and negative connotations. A loner can be someone who doesn't quite fit in, who stays by himself and doesn't socialize at all. A loner can be a popular person, too, with friends and all the traditional positive societal trappings, someone who is simply different in a private way. How does this, the first and most important trait to separate young successes from the average achiever, become apparent?

Alan Dershowitz, who at age 28 became the youngest full professor in the history of Harvard Law School, is one sort of loner whose background wouldn't appear to preordain him for success. According to him, at 18 he was a "failure." He had few friends, a 68 average in high school, and girls in his lower-income Brooklyn neighborhood were forbidden to go out with him. He was constantly suspended from school for being aggressive and a smart aleck. The more his peers avoided him or made fun of him, the more aggressive he became. Teachers, peers and family told him he was a failure.

They also told him he should be a lawyer, for he was "stupid and verbal." Such a background fueled an "I'll show you" attitude. Dershowitz, who had not been known for his scholarship in high school, in his senior year scored among the highest in his class on college entrance exams. He won a scholarship (his teachers, baffled, accused him of cheating) to Brooklyn College, where he graduated magna cum laude. He then worked his way through Yale Law School, graduating magna cum laude again. His loner status was fueled by the fact that Dershowitz felt he "saw things a little differently than other people—that's a vice in high school but a virtue at Yale Law School." Part of his separation was induced by a strict family, part was simply the result of feeling different from others. What enabled him to succeed, to the point that he is now one of the premier constitutional lawyers in America? He says it's because:

> "There's a certain kind of smart I'm not. It's the kind of smart that was rewarded in high school. I'm still not that kind of smart. What I've been able to do and what other successful people have been able to do is to be able to evaluate your own type of smarts and then make the world believe that the right question is the one that you're best able to answer. It's being able to shape the ballpark around your abilities."

In other words, Alan Dershowitz made his loner-ness into an asset, applying it to his work instead of letting it work against him.

Dick Ebersol was a loner, too, but in an entirely different way. On the surface, he would appear to be a "once-born"—

his family was close, his upbringing in pastoral Connecticut fairly comfortable. He had a close family relationship and was quietly encouraged to excel. He went to Yale, but left in his sophomore year to become a television sports "gofer" and researcher (three years later, he returned to finish up his degree). For all his conventional comfort, Ebersol thought himself somehow different. His instincts as an "outsider" served him well; he helped develop the popular and iconoclastic "Saturday Night Live" on television. By the time he was 28, he had been named the youngest vice president in the history of NBC. Ebersol says that his drive "came from a combination of supportive parents and enjoying being by myself. If you are a loner, you have two ways of going: either you become a pinball wizard or you think up ideas. I thought up ideas."

Lucinda Franks was a classic loner. She used to live in a world of her own. While other children were playing baseball, she was in her room reading Sartre. She enjoyed reading more than playing. She rebelled against her comfortable, middle-class upbringing, finding her niche in writing. Her intense drive was born of a separation from those her own age:

> "I spent a fairly lonely childhood. I took things more seriously than most kids. I guess I was more sensitive. I wasn't that good at sports, so I spent a lot of time alone in my room with 'South Pacific' blasting on the record player, trying to sing with it. I had a strong urge at an early age to be somebody. I felt isolated. I thought, 'someday, I'll show them!'"

For Franks, being a loner heightened her perceptions of the world around her and brought an added sensitivity to her writing. These qualities helped her, at age 24, to win the Pulitzer Prize for investigative reporting. Her story: an insightful series on the radical underground movement of the Sixties.

Ted Chin's sense of isolation was more cultural. He was literally raised in two cultures—an aggressive, accomplishment-

centered Western society, and his family's Eastern heritage of
reflection and spontaneity. The strong influence of his family's
belief in excellence made him somehow "older" than his peers:

> "Every night after school I went off to private school
> where I was tutored in Chinese, history, philosophy, callig-
> raphy, reading the characters and a touch of judo. I resented it
> because it would take time away from the normal things you
> would do—playing baseball or running off to a movie or just
> doing nothing. I felt different from other children. I think I
> had a greater sense of standards. I always wanted to achieve
> more, accomplish more. I was a bit more mature and more
> of a loner than most."

Chin was popular in school and had many friends. But he was
nonetheless different from his playmates. Such a vantage point,
reached by positive separation with benefit of social and peer
acceptance, helped Chin to succeed. At 27 he was made the
youngest vice president in the history of Benton and Bowles
advertising agency, and today, just a few years later, owns and
runs a highly profitable and innovative New York agency.

For Steven Markoff, the separation was born of disappointment at his peers' and his parents' inability to grasp his interests:

> "I thought I had a different set of eyes. I would look and
> see something and everybody else would look and not see. I
> had my own company because I couldn't get along with most
> of the other kids. They were out stealing hubcaps and I was
> doing business deals."

Those business deals began at age 11, when he bought a
Buffalo head nickel for twice the amount it was worth and became interested in coins. Coins became his hobby, and, eventually, his business. His parents, living in a lower-middle-class
section of Los Angeles, "never quite understood" their son's
goals. Markoff went to junior college near his home, then left
to found his own business. Today Markoff is 33; his A-Mark

Coin company is one of the leading U.S. wholesalers of gold and silver coins and bullion. His company, which he built from scratch, does more than $100 million in sales each year.

Joe Armstrong managed to make his loner qualities work for him with his peers. Armstrong had a close and warm relationship with his family, but suffered the lack of peer acceptance common to young successes. So his early projects were practical ones for helping to pay the family bills: he'd sell donuts and magazines door to door, or cut, haul and sell cords of wood. Attending high school was rough for Armstrong, who remembers with the vividness of one who was never with the "in" group:

> "I was very out. I remember being very unhappy. In Abilene you had to be good-looking and had to be a football player to be in any way accepted, and I wasn't. I had an old '42 Plymouth station wagon and I remember having to go sit in it and eat my lunch by myself. I'm an 'outie,' I guess, but I'm proud of it."

Attending college in his home state of Texas changed that a bit. Armstrong's natural enthusiasm and sensitivity made up for his lack of money and athletic stature and brought him honors and popularity. Still, that initial feeling of estrangement fed his drive. At 33, as publisher of *Rolling Stone* magazine, he became the youngest person ever to place on a prominent consumer magazine executives list. At 34, he was named President and Editor-in-Chief of *New York* Magazine Company.

———

Most young successes were loners from the start, or became loners while still in their early school years. Yet at the same time, they developed very strong ties to the adults around them, be those adults parents, relatives or family friends. All the young successes interviewed mentioned that they were more comfortable with adults than children their own age while growing up, and that seems to have carried over to their contemporary lives. Many of the men had dated and continue to date—or marry—women who are older. Many of the women successes dated or married older men. Many of the friendships that were important to them in their early years were with those children who were a few classes ahead. A common theme was that of "growing up too fast," or simply feeling somehow more mature than other children. In such a situation, an adult figure becomes doubly important. The presence of an influential adult figure— in a positive or negative sense—is a second major factor contributing to the making of an early bloomer.

For many of the women, the father was an important influence. Patricia DeBlank, a successful Wall Street veteran, who at age 31 manages a 2-billion-dollar customer account in the government bond market, was strongly influenced by her father. He was a businessman, and gave her constant encouragement. Eric Berne's "script" theory of motivation fits DeBlank's experience. From the time she was able to comprehend, she was told that she was as smart as anybody else and that whatever she decided she wanted to do she would be able to figure out a way to do it. With that sound running through her head, she simply went out and did just that: she achieved.

Variations on DeBlank's script are to be found in many young successes. Many women and men were close to their fathers. Most of the men stress the tempering qualities of their mothers, speaking of their mother's empathetic "female" qualities, which balanced a hard-driving or business-minded father. The women were close to their fathers as well, but whether this influence of the father on the lives of young successful women will shift as more mothers take their place in the active workforce and as more female role models emerge remains to be seen. The mothers of these men and women were, for the most part, from a generation when women did not work outside the home or, if they did, did so for a limited period of time and not as a step leading to a career.

Fathers were especially important, however, to the men. Often this inherently volatile relationship was cause for early trauma, and the already existing father/son competition was heightened. Either the pressured script for the men read "succeed and don't fail like your father" or "succeed just as I have." Many of the men were living examples of Freud's concept of eternal struggle for power between parent and child. Some men felt guilty about their relationships with their fathers —but not for traditional reasons. These early successes felt uncomfortable because they had succeeded far more than their fathers ever did or could have, and at a younger age as well. "My father had good people skills but little business sense," said one successful corporate executive, almost apologetically. He echoed the thoughts of many of those interviewed. Others said, with some bitterness, that their fathers had had great business acumen but little empathy in dealing with others.

There were, of course, some who were influenced by fathers who were quietly driven men setting positive examples for their offspring. One young business magnate, who has a close and warm relationship with his stepfather, nevertheless still feels the presence—"like a guardian angel"—of his real father, who died when he was five. This vision has become a strong motivator in his drive for success. The influences of adults—positively or negatively—were strongly felt by both men and women. Where they were unable to be close to their parents, a family friend or older relative helped set an example and became a friend at the same time. The facility to make friends with those who were older, to be in the same league holding one's own while at the same time learning "older" things, is finely honed in those who become early achievers. In almost every case, the young men and women who achieved have already exceeded the success level of their parents.

———

How does this capacity to deal with the elders pay off, and where does it fit in with a pattern of accomplishment at an early age? Lee Eisenberg became the editor of *Esquire* at age 29:

> I made a veritable career of saying "I'm just a kid." I used it, I really did. I would try to be wide-eyed. I know my personality wasn't such that it was terribly believable—I don't think I was ever wimpy enough to pull that off successfully—but I thought I did and it gave me another weapon to defend myself. It made embarrassment a little easier.

David Obst knows what Eisenberg is talking about. At 31, Obst has already had a stunningly successful career as a literary agent (Woodward and Bernstein, two other early achievers, were among his clients) and today runs his own division of Random House. Like Eisenberg, Obst had no particular financial or social advantages to help out in a career. But like Eisenberg, Obst had that special facility to find the person in charge—and learn from him:

> "I had the capacity to be able to deal with older men in such a way as to have them tell me everything they know without feeling threatened that I was going to come after them and devour them from behind. There's a certain kind of person who can deal with older men and have those older men feel that they can tell and trust them and teach them in such a way as not to be threatened by them. It has happened to me everywhere I've gone. Because of my youth and inexperience they could have taken enormous advantage of me and didn't. Instead they taught me. And I'm appreciative of it."

The ability to use their youth constructively is the third important factor for young success. Absent to great degree in these early bloomers is that great folly of youth, the belief that one knows everything there is to know. To the contrary, young successes make a career of finding out what they do not know, and of finding the right people to inform them of same. Sometimes that person becomes a mentor. A mentor could be someone who simply gives a hopeful a chance to do something, or a person who guides many aspects of one's career. If a young success type does have such a champion, it is not for long. It is highly unusual for a young overachiever to stay with a mentor throughout his or her career. Indeed, all those interviewed who did have a mentor had not one, but at least two and as many as six along their short rise to the top.

Mentors are important to some people's fast career climb, but not all-important. These young career hotshots who made it to the top without a corporate parent figure are plentiful and, it turns out, many of them at the ripe old age of 26 or 30 are now themselves playing mentor to younger counterparts, giving those young ones the benefit of the mentor relationship the young success never had. If a mentor is not in the wings, a young success does not sit weeping in the corner, waiting for one to show up. Instead, he or she creates mini-mentors. Take Memphis millionaire Ira Lipman, who at 34 has built from scratch one of this country's leading security service companies. When he was starting out he would read business journal accounts about successful typcoons and entrepreneurs—and he would call them up and ask for an appointment. Lipman didn't have a mentor, someone with whom to compare aspirations and from whom to glean advice. So he flew to where the expertise was, getting audiences with prominent, established achievers. During these discussions he would pose questions about the mistakes the tycoons had made, and tell them of his mistakes. Flattered by the attention and solidly entrenched in business enough not to view Lipman as a competitor, such men would open up with advice, warnings, hints and good conversation.

Other young successes *sans* mentors follow Lipman's pattern. They are eager for seasoned advice, open to different points of view. They not only hear the experiences of others—they listen. This eagerness to learn separates them from their average achiever

counterparts who are loath to admit mistakes. When Lipman
was called to make a speech before a distinguished gathering of
southern kingpins and found he was the youngest man there,
he took off his coat and spoke about every mistake he had ever
made in business. He was, it goes without saying, a hit with the
group.

＝＝

R. Stephen Lefler has a short attention span. He's always
doing several projects at once, and in college this habit was already firmly entrenched. While going to school in Texas, he
held down several jobs that to other people would be full-time
employment. Putting himself through school, Lefler worked
eighty hours a week at a newspaper, in retail advertising. He
handled accounts that could be called on during the evening. In
his "spare" time, he wrote newspaper filler stories and short
stories in addition to his school work. His senior year in college,
he earned $25,000. He was accepted at Harvard Business School
for graduate study, and four years later was named, at age 27,
the president of DesignResearch, Inc.

It is common to hear young successes like Lefler talk about
their short attention spans—in positive terms. For what seems
to most of us to be a negative trait (we describe people as
"scatterbrained," "unable to concentrate," or "fickle"), young
achievers turn into an asset. Attention spans from "thirty sec-
onds" to "three minutes" seem to be the most popular among
this bunch, and the restlessness that gives birth to such a scat-
tering of resources is the fourth trait that separates young successes from average achievers. In high school and college (for
some, as early as grammar school) these people were possessed
of an energy surplus that found its outlet in outside interests.
Many, like Lefler, formed their own college businesses, or worked
for others while earning a degree at the same time. By the time
many of these people had hit their teens, they were old pros at

organizing people and organizations. Some became mini-entrepreneurs. And from an early age, they showed ingenuity. No simple lemonade stands for them—Joe Armstrong, for instance, in grammar school used to send for free telephone company educational films and then charge the neighborhood kids a nickel to view them. School work alone couldn't fill the achievers' time or catch their interests. Young successes take great delight in running down the list of jobs they have held, from the cradle on. That list is more often than not incredibly varied, for almost all of the young achievers had to work for a living from the time they were in high school.

Their restlessness leads to a striving unique among early achievers. Lynn D. Salvage parlayed a knowledge of international finance and a Harvard MBA into a Bankers Trust vice presidency at age 29. One year later she was named president of the First Woman's Bank, making her the youngest bank president in the country. One of the reasons she got there so fast was an unusual view of herself shared by others who become successful young:

> Where you see me as an achiever I see myself as all the things I still haven't achieved. I'm never satisfied with myself. Success is always a few steps ahead. I'm really at my best when I've got one hundred things to do and not enough hours in the day to do them.

This restlessness, this drive, often shows up in frequent job hops. Where many would spend five years in a job before leaving, a young success might spend two . . . and in some cases, one. When things get dull or do not provide the satisfaction that was promised, the young achiever usually hightails it to the next challenge . . . and the next. Norman W. Spaulding, Jr., at 30 years of age is today a successful and innovative business administrator. As general manager of a California shopping complex with $33 million in annual sales, he is known for his ability to organize and make decisions. But a study of his earlier business career would seem to be a study in nomadism. In 1966, he was a premed student at Lake Forest college in Illinois—there were doctors on both sides of his family and he thought he'd become one, too. But in his senior year, he decided being a doctor was not for him, and he enrolled at the University of Iowa Law School. A year later, he realized he didn't like lawyers' work, and left for Mexico with his wife for six months to think things through. He returned to the United States with a wife and a new baby daughter, moved in with his in-laws and took a $2.50-an-hour marine construction job. In his spare time he began looking for a way to break into the corporate structure. When he did finally get a job, as a project planner for Mattel, Inc., he was so poor that when his car broke down on the way to his new location, Spaulding had to spend a month working in a gas station in order to get it repaired.

The wandering paid off for Spaulding, who worked hard and was given more and more responsibility. But when his employer refused to promote him because "they were concerned about how some of their major clients might respond to my being Black," Spaulding left. He began his own company, then joined Montgomery Ward for two years (pulling down four promotions in the process). Then he hopped to the Eastmont shopping complex in Oakland, which he turned into a raving success. With each unsure turn of the road, Spaulding reflects the spirit of young achievers in one important area: he knew what job wasn't for him, had the courage to leave, and had the intelligence to profit in some way by each.

Spaulding's story is not untypical of early achievers. The restlessness inherent in the breed is not just fickle flightiness, impatience or an absence of stick-to-it-ness. If impatience is there—and it frequently is—it is coupled with the desire to do more, to work harder than one is working. The "by their works ye shall know them" school of thought cannot be stressed enough in the study of young success. The desire to work hard and the ability to work hard turns restlessness into productivity —and progress.

This willingness to work is the fifth crucial factor in the early achievement roadmap. Without exception, these quickly-bored horizon seekers mentioned hard work as the reason for their being able to translate the rest of their experiences into success. More than just mentioning hard work, they dwell upon it. They are proud of the fact they had worked for what they had. Nothing was ever given to them: they did not inherit their positions or businesses, but had to work and fight for them. For they have an instinctive mistrust of being given things; they consider a thing valuable only if some self-motivated sweat went into its acquisition. New ideas or Sixties approaches to the subject notwithstanding, the ethic of working for what one has is important to them. Each mentioned the satisfaction—for some, a joy—born of hard work. Some of the young successes could be defined as workaholics; indeed, some define themselves this way. But overworkers or not, all genuinely like to work hard and are uncomfortable when they cannot. They could no more relax in one corporate or personal way station and coast through life effortlessly than they could be happy being merely "one of the gang" in high school. Treading water just isn't in their nature.

> • I've had some events take place in my life which really jolted me and made me realize I wasn't in control. When I was 26 years old, three weeks to the day I was supposed to get married, my fiancée died of a brain tumor. That really affected me.
>
> —William George, who at 30 was named president of one of Litton Industries largest divisions; today at 36 he is the youngest corporate vice president in the history of Litton Industries.
>
> • My father's death was a very traumatic thing and I think in large measure I'm where I am today because I saw my

mother totally traumatized. To see your mother crying when she's been strong, blows your sense of security. My sister and I are probably more driven than our brothers in that we do not want to have the same thing happen to us.

—Jennifer Siebens, 24-year-old producer for CBS

• You are greatly enriched if you understand what happened to you. Everybody should go into the army for a minimum of six months, everybody should be mugged once in their life. As we go through this little rat maze we get mugged, beaten, destroyed by our parents, our friends. Everything that can happen, happens. Then you look back and say, Jesus those were interesting experiences. You have to pay to play.

—Steven Markoff

Whether it be the death of a family member or loved one, the presence of a "great hurt" inflicted by others somewhere along the line, or hard knocks in general, a sixth element found in the lives of young successes is that of early seasoning. Tragedy in many cases begets such seasoning, and can come in forms large and small. Many men and women mentioned the death of their fathers as a turning point in their lives. The death of a parent profoundly affected the lives of the superachievers. Such a trauma made the impression upon them that time was fleeting, that there was only a limited time in which to accomplish what they wished to accomplish. Achievement was spurred in others by suicide attempts by close friends or the achievers' own brushes with danger or death. The end result of each was a sense of urgency.

The school of hard knocks and its contributions toward seasoning cannot be minimized. In many cases, a young success will bring it upon himself—restlessness results in experimentation, the taking of risk, myriad number of jobs and experiences. All contribute to a greater sense of self. Self-knowledge is an important element in the success of an overachiever. It is linked to having one's feet on the ground, to being street-wise, to knowing what one is capable of, to greater self-awareness. This self-knowledge enables an achiever to take risks where others fear, to see obstacles that stop others not as obstacles, but as challenges. Few interviewed were *not* touched by an element of personal tragedy. Theirs, as a breed, is the ability to learn from such things, to transcend their fears.

———

The young successes of the Seventies had a seventh element to season their lives that other generations had not: the Sixties. While most young successes interviewed were not active participants in the demonstrations and protest that characterized those years, the turmoil and upheaval of those years did have a marked effect on their brand of success. Those achievers who believed in what all the noise was about expressed their support, for the most part, not by marching, but by being sympathetic observers, organizing behind the scenes. Even those not sympathetic to the causes were profoundly affected by the times and found it difficult to balance their beliefs with what was going on around them.

Leon Botstein in 1970 became the nation's youngest college president, age 23, when he took the helm at Franconia College, New Hampshire. Today, at 30, he is president of Bard College in New York, and is still the nation's youngest college president. The Sixties were a difficult time for Botstein and others of his generation:

> It was a tumultuous period emotionally because you were constantly sorting this stuff out. The lure of really radical involvement was always there. A lot of my friends disappeared. Some went underground. My first girlfriend in grad school, the brightest student in the history department, vanished. You struggled with the issues. It was very hard. At the same time I had tremendous interest in intellectual issues, but hardly the peace and quiet to think these things through in a serious way.

I couldn't entertain the idea that one could somehow con-
template the inner reaches of art, society and scholarship while
Rome literally burns.

But were the Sixties that profound, in retrospect? Lee Eisenberg thinks they were—and that he has an edge because of
them:

> I think the times were far more oppressive and frighten-
> ing than they are now. We went through a hell of a lot. If you
> went through it and emerged from it, you emerged so much
> stronger. I think there is a way of seeing the worst. You know
> you're not going to see it that bad anymore. Therefore you have
> a lot more strength and drive to go on and get about your life
> and do well. I weathered my father's death, a suicide and the
> Sixties. Nothing scares me.

The Sixties' concern with power and achievement was a
negative concern: people who had become successes were usually
part of the Establishment, and the Establishment (whatever it
was), along with those who had aspirations to power, was defi-
nitely Out. Those young sympathetic achievers who had in them
the desire for success and power were on the outs, too. They
had to keep such drive and ambition to themselves, or channel
their energy into more popular causes to keep from coming out
on the side of said Establishment.

But there were some who could use the Sixties to their advantage, just as they used their youth. For David Obst, the
Sixties:

> ...made being young so respectable because of media per-
> ceptions of what we were doing and how hip and in and fun it
> was. Jesus, what kind of literary agent could show up in a
> MacDonald's blazer, tennis shoes and an American flag tie?
> That was my standard outfit for the first three years I did
> business. Everybody said, "well, yeah, you're eccentric but
> that's the way young people are today." It was totally accepted,
> and I guess it helped.

It helped, all right, helped to steer young achievers—whether by seasoning, stereotyping or shaking up—toward their goals. And wanting to make it became a silent goal of a Sixties generation of achievers. Some, like Lucinda Franks, straddled the Establishment and anti-Establishment by becoming journalists; professional observers. Others, like adman Ted Chin, were sympathetic to the spirit of the times but worked busily within the system. Chin tried as a college student in Boston to improve the curriculum, the faculty and educational opportunities for minorities at his university.

Whatever the individual reaction, the young success story was altered by the Sixties. Because of the Sixites, the young no longer had to apologize for being young. As we will see later, the way business was done was changed. The avenues to achievement were altered. And as we will also see later, if the Sixties did open up more opportunities for young success, offered more seasoning for an achiever's drive, then those years also compounded the many problems that young overachievers have.

———

What makes it happen? And what can make it happen for you? As we have seen, there are seven major factors that contribute to early achievement. But does that mean that if you are a loner, have strong early ties and camaraderie with adults, are able to have your youth be an asset and not threaten potential mentors, are restless, thrive on hard work, have some crisis which left you with a "life is fleeting" feeling, and were deeply affected by the Sixties that you are assured of being the next president of General Motors at age 25?

That would be nice, but the success formula is not that easy. Not every achiever possessed all seven elements at once. Different combinations worked for different people. David Obst was able to use his Sixties eccentricities to make him more visible to publishers as a literary agent. At the same time he was able to cultivate and learn from powerful older men who could teach him and not be threatened by his talent and ambition or put off by his strange apparel. Steven Markoff was a classic loner who could only be comfortable working in a business that was his alone. His crisis—the slights of his peers and the apparent inability of his parents to grasp his personal complexities—gave him an added dimension of depth and sensitivity. Patricia DeBlank combined a strong positive family influence with a basic restlessness. Ted Chin, living in two cultures, had at the same time strong, respectful ties to his elders while feeling older and more innovative than his peers. Ira Lipman felt "older," too, and was able to use his youth to his advantage when cultivating mentors. He also describes himself as a "workaholic." Jennifer Siebens was lucky to have a mentor in college who believed in her television production ability; she also had the crisis of her father's death to fuel her desires to achieve. Many combinations can work.

Yet those traits, coupled with the intense desire to achieve and excel, still cannot by themselves create young success. Those fragile, amorphous qualities of luck and chemistry enter into the picture. Perhaps David Obst might not have been able to cultivate a strong mentor if the man in question simply didn't like his youth–culture style. He was fortunate, however, to meet men who did click with his business technique and who happened to believe in his ideas and talent. Lee Eisenberg entered an *Esquire* writing contest while still a college student. He entered at the spur of the moment and almost as an afterthought. He won his trip to New York as a junior editor at *Esquire* and his fast-track magazine career was launched. What would have happened if he hadn't been quite up to writing that day? Would his career have zoomed, or would he have finished his Communications degree and ended up an intelligent university communications professor of average tenured age?

Can you ever *plan* success? Or do you simply "luck" into it, spreading your arms happily as success comes by to embrace you at random? It is an almost unchartable combination of the two that brings success. For those interviewed, both luck and planning entered into the picture to varying degrees. Some felt that their planning paid off: Lynn Salvage purposely went into international banking because she knew that there were few women in the field and that she would therefore become more visible; Ira Lipman saw that shoplifting and other crime was on the rise and noted correctly that the potential market for private security guards would expand in coming years. Both Salvage and Lipman were ready for success, backed up by personal research and the ability to know when to use their talents. But others felt they had been in the proverbial right place at the right time: one woman banking official applied to a large institution at the same time that that institution had been instructed to hire more women, unbeknownst to her; Dick Ebersol instinctively felt that the viewing audience would be responsible to an ir-reverent, topical live comedy show. Timing—not necessarily planning—was important in these cases.

Certainly, luck and planning, in and of themselves, can only take you so far. There are an equal or greater number of factors, too, that can stop success: bad timing, a poor economy, an employer who doesn't believe in your talents or simply doesn't like you, being in the wrong field at the wrong time, being in the wrong field altogether. With such variables also going against many young successes, how did these young successes get there? Not all of them set out to become young wizards—indeed, many are still somewhat in awe of the fact that they have come as far and as fast as they have. Many became success-ful in fields they had never planned to be in in the first place. Even those who did plan were faced with the same roadblocks and circumstances that each of us face in our desire to achieve, to Be Somebody.

So what made success happen? Maybe these people were

happy with adults, were loners, restless, hard working, sensitive and pushed by the Sixties. And maybe they had a good dose of luck and planning to reach their goals. Maybe they had some of these traits but not all of them. But regardless of the combination or combinations of factors inherent in each individual, each of these individuals had one important, overriding characteristic that made it happen for him or her: each was able to see opportunity and each was not afraid to grab it—or, if he or she was afraid, grabbed it anyway. Luck, planning and childhood trauma can only take one so far. The rest of the way depends on your abilities, sensibilities and perceptions—the awareness with which the whole package is put together. Each young success had the ability to shape that ballpark around his or her talents, to know what those special talents and perceptions were so that when opportunity—planned or lucky—came along it could be utilized.

In the doing, of course, the achievers took tremendous risks. But they took those risks knowing that there was simply no other way, knowing that each new opportunity, while it offered with it a chance for loss, also offered a chance for growth and success. That chance to grow, to change—even in the face of the fear that always comes with change—was too strong to resist. They took the risks. They grabbed the opportunity. And they won.

# 4 ≣ The Status Dilemma

THE WINNING of success—especially early success—
brings with it position, prestige, monetary gain and seemingly
unbridled opportunity. We see someone who is blessed with
both youth and achievement and think them quite lucky.
Looking at an early bloomer, seeing the exterior trappings of
success and outward manifestations of inward self-confidence,
it is hard to imagine that good fortune has a negative side. We
think someone who is successful while young has security,
wealth and power. Some of them do, of course. But if an
achiever has all these magical things, he or she also has many
special problems. Ironically, to some degree many of these
difficulties are common to the average or even below-average
achiever. For superachievers, however, the problems are writ
large.

Success can be a cause for celebration and smugness. Who
wouldn't want to have a nice place to live, a great car to drive

and a fat bank account, plus the energy to enjoy it all? But those things can have a dark side and become cause for professional and social jealousy and envy. Thomas Grojean knows that—at 37 he became president and chief executive officer of Tiger Leasing Corporation. It was unusual for someone so young to assume such a position even a few years ago, and Grojean immediately encountered the young success version of the Double Whammy. "If you hire a guy who is twenty-nine and he strikes out, people say: 'You should have known because he's only a kid,'" Grojean says. "If he's forty and he strikes out, they say: 'You win some and you lose some.'" Grojean won his battle, but he and other achievers must and do realize that such discomfort comes with the attainment territory.

In many ways, a young achiever's troubles are just beginning when he or she reaches that professorship, editorship, vice presidency or first million. Many of these troubles, as we shall see later, are self-generated—insecurities, inexperience, adjustments and fears that come from within the individual as reactions to, or driving forces toward, success. Steven Markoff, who became rich at an age when most of his contemporaries were slugging it out in business school, wrestles perpetually with such self-generated problems. He is not alone in this group:

> I think it's unhealthy to become a businessman at eleven years old. If my kid ever did that I'd beat the hell out of him. I think that people who have our mentality go through an incredible unsettling of the terrain. Maybe we never see the frivolous years. And I think, as a romanticist, that everybody should have them. Success is the bleeding—the wound came much earlier.

But many of the difficulties young successes can experience come from external sources—coworkers, friends, family, older and younger superiors and subordinates. Such people feel threatened, left behind, confused. Lee Eisenberg experienced such a problem when he was at *Esquire*. And even though it was disguised with good humor, the unusual message came through:

> After I was made editor, the president of the publishing division said, "Is it really true you're twenty-nine? That's really embarrassing. You're not embarrassed, but don't you think the world will think it's pretty silly?" And I said, "I sure do, because it sounds really silly to me." He half-jokingly said, "Can't you lie and say you're thirty-three?"

The more somber aspects of early achievement seem to be about equally divided between external and internal sources. Given this state of affairs, it is not surprising to find most young achievers on the professional defensive. Many of those interviewed mentioned a sense of social and personal isolation as a result. They speak of a need to be always alert to the manipulations of others. And they have had to cultivate a great sensitivity to those who are less accomplished. These mechanisms are necessities, not luxuries. They are needed if the achiever wants to keep on achieving, or even stay in the same place. A fact of life is that the young achiever will be sniped at on the way to the top and bombarded when the apex is finally reached. Resentment, in obvious or subtle form, is omnipresent, and if one is to remain successful for the long term, one has to learn to deal with it early.

Resentment of the early success of others is understandable. Who isn't miffed and disappointed when it doesn't happen to us—either not as fast as we'd like, or not at all? The young charger poses a threat, just as anyone who does not quite conform to our idea of the norm—in a positive or negative way—will tend to do.

It isn't necessary to be a full-fledged young success to generate such umbrage, either. Just the promise of being different is often enough to draw the battle lines. In its June, 1977, issue, *Fortune* listed the potential roadblocks bright young MBA graduates would be finding in business. In describing the market for such eager graduates as existing within the boundaries of a "love–hate relationship," it revealed some problems inherent in being a young success type. The older controller or executive who has been in business thirty years, for instance, fears the sophisticated skills of the new graduate. The MBA education is often far advanced from what the older man has known. Yet at the same time, the older executive knows that the skills of the new MBA are the skills of the future. He can pass up the youngster and take a chance on being left behind, or can hire him or her and take a chance on being replaced. As with the MBA, the earliest challenge for a young success is getting hired in the first place. Surmounting the "He/She's too young and consequently what can he or she know about running a business/ teaching/editing/the law?" barrier is hard enough. But surmounting the "He/She is sharp and will eat me alive . . . or will at least diminish my power" barrier is the acid test, a taste of trauma to come.

Even in a time of rapid change, it is not easy for those members of the baby-boom generation to make their presence felt. One basic obstacle stands in the way of young people hoping to assume positions of responsibility, stands even in the way of those highly self-directed and motivated people who become young success stories. That barrier is the specter of the generation gap. Nowhere has evidence of that gap surfaced with such strength as in a survey published by *Industry Week* in 1975. The magazine had asked more than 550 readers where the under-forty manager was taking industry. Did he or she make a difference? Twenty-six percent of the readers polled were themselves managers under forty. Thirty-seven percent were in the 40 to 50 age bracket, and thirty-seven percent were older than 50 years of age. With such a diverse age spread, some strong conclusions were reached about what younger managers could and could not do. The trend toward younger managers in business was a given. Within this context, a majority of *Industry Week's* respondents agreed that young managers worked harder these days and were more effective in their jobs than young managers of the past who did not have the advantages of today's sophisticated business education. All surveyed seemed to agree that young managers were more flexible in their management style and more capable of change than their older counterparts. There was no doubt that such youthful businessmen and women questioned the whys, wherefores, and how-to's of their jobs, and their company's practices, with a keen and studied eye. Perhaps because of the turmoil of the Sixties and the imposed consciousness of that period of time—whether or not one agreed with the demonstration of the week—today's young managers were found to be more socially aware, more involved than their older business peers. Their new style and involvement in social and civic issues were viewed by the respondents as being an effective tool to change for the good the image of American business.

However, when asked to compare today's older managers, those between 40 and 50, with the under-forty manager of today, those polled voted in strong majority in favor of the elders. The respondents said that the young manager, in their opinion, is not as well equipped, because he or she lacks the key element of time-tested experience. Perhaps the young manager has had a more sophisticated course of study, but to be effective, the poll concluded, something more is needed. If a young manager can condense ten years experience into three that's fine, but nothing can substitute for the valuable element of time. By a margin of 53 percent to 45 percent, the respondents found today's younger managers more effective than the older managers were when they were younger. But the survey noted that older employees—and even some younger ones—still felt psychologically more comfortable working for an older employer.

The generation gap extended all the way to the bottom line,

that measure which not only indicates which business is doing well and which isn't, but which also separates effective management style from the ineffective. The majority of the *Industry Week* respondents, regardless of age, indicated they felt those managers between the ages of 40 and 50 were the most likely to be profit-oriented. Recognizing this difference, however, 86 percent of the young managers polled voted "yes" when asked if the under-forty executive *should* be as profit oriented as older managers. With the use of the survey, charting the differences between the generations became a somewhat easier task than in the past. While there would be exceptions to each category, in the main managers over fifty years of age could be termed strictly bottom-line oriented in their management style. Managers between 40 and 50 would seem to be profit-motivated with a touch of people-orientation. And perhaps as a reflection of the times in which they came of age, the under-forty manager would tend to be strongly people oriented. The bottom line is never forgotten, but depending on the age bracket of the manager, that line has been tempered.

Such a poll helps to define the battle lines of age. These lines, though slowly being conquered, are still very much a part of business and social life. The impatience, hard work, energy and skepticism of youth will no more change than the insistence on experience and patience (as well as the skepticism of the new) that comes with age. Yet within that battle, something has changed. There exists a new realization that the young are taking places in management and business that previously had not been open to them. The sheer shortage of managers in the 40 to 50 and over-fifty age brackets has made today's under-forty generation responsible—and in large numbers. That, and a given generation gap for starters, have made the atmosphere markedly different.

Yet, a young success is automatically thrust into a position where he or she must constantly prove worthiness. And within this burden of proof is the tacit understanding that the successful achiever will be "older" than his or her years. Bard College president, Leon Botstein, felt the pressure when he was made president of Franconia College at 23:

> One of the difficult things about being in a position of so-called achievement—external achievement—at a young age is that you're expected to possess not so much answers but a well-constructed opinion of the world. You have to speak in an authoritative tone, and admitting your ignorance or uncertainty is relatively incompatible with the job. You can go through a process of self-delusion, that you do in fact have the answers and your knowldege of the situation is as if you had seen this for thirty years. The younger you get into the job the greater the temptation to imitate. The tension is there because you feel inadequate to some extent. You try to think "what are the sort of formal exteriors of this kind of job?" How do you look like you're the bank president at a young age?

No matter how well grounded a young success is, how steeped in self-knowledge, the temptation to adopt such formal exteriors is quite strong. Many of those interviewed, such as Harvard Law Professor Alan Dershowitz, bowed to such images for a time:

> There were people who came to see me and said, "Look, I know you deserve tenure but don't you think you should put it off a couple of years just because it would make people somewhat more comfortable?" I wasn't prepared to do that. I resent tremendously the fact that I was forced to become older, quicker. I look back at pictures of myself at age twenty-eight and twenty-nine and I really looked forty in those pictures. I dressed like I was forty. There was tremendous pressure on me from colleagues and peers. Such pressures made me really not enjoy a period of time between twenty-eight and thirty-two because unconsciously I accepted their insistences and became older. I wasted my life going to those goddamned

dinner parties where all these old people were sitting around talking old things and I would out-old them. There came a point where I said why the hell should I behave so much older when I'm so much younger...getting older made me want to be younger and appreciate the virtues of youth.

Appreciating the virtues of youth is a problem frequently mentioned by those interviewed. The "I lost my childhood, damnit" syndrome is very strong in many young achievers. It is not meant to be synonymous with having an unhappy childhood (relatively few of the achievers described themselves as miserable while young), it is nevertheless a source of some sadness in hindsight. Being older than one's years while a child leaves its mark. Many felt hesitant or unmoved at all to participate in the traditional "follies of youth." The silliness, frivolity that everyone else seemed to be having had passed them by. Sooner than expected, perhaps because they were unaccepted by peers, the achievers found themselves running with older crowds, associating with people whose aims and intelligence were more on a par with their own. This, while providing some seasoning for their later accomplishments, also left a bittersweet gap.

Some young successes played on their youth as they got older, using the traditional cockiness of their age as a springboard—and a defense. As mentioned earlier, David Obst wore a Mac-Donald's blazer and American flag tie instead of literary tweeds. Such duds were both a statement and a badge. Ted Chin admits that in his advertising career he was a bit brassy at the beginning, charging ahead in business decisions where more sensitive or cautious managers would exercise care and patience. As a vice president of Benton and Bowles at 27, Chin began sending senior management regular monthly reports on how it could improve business. While such brashness didn't impress the elders of the firm—and may even have served to intimidate them and put them off—one of his suggestions was successfully tried. That suggestion was to bring in a trainer to teach young executives the skills they would need to take over the business in ten to twenty years. As part of the program, professionally conducted sensitivity sessions were held. As a result of feedback from his older colleagues at these sessions, Chin realized he needed to exercise a greater sense of tolerance, patience and tact with his older coworkers and superiors if he was to peacefully—and successfully—coexist with them.

California businessman Norman Spaulding was almost done in by his brashness. On the job in Mattel's marketing department, he "didn't have enough sense not to embarrass my boss in meetings. If he had forgotten to do something, I said so. If I thought his conclusions were erroneous, I would say so." While there was little argument as to Spaulding's dedication, abilities and gutsiness, it was possible that an excess of chutzpah could have held him back. Labeled "abrasive" and "unwilling to play the corporate game" (a danger for young success loners), he became unpopular with his immediate supervisors and coworkers. Fortunately, the division president recognized that Spaulding's talent could be channeled in sales. His brashness and his boss's faith paid off—in two years, sales in his new territory leaped from $200,000 to $2 million.

If that division president had been threatened by Spaulding, or if Benton and Bowles senior management had been intimidated by Chin, the stories could have been different—at least in the short term. Having mentors or superiors who can recognize that under a flurry of inappropriate memos lurks a real talent is an important counterbalance to young-success impatience. Such recognition is important to anyone—super- or average achiever—and can't always be planned. The "brashness factor" isn't entirely negative, of course; it can be inherently charming and forgiveable in a young talent. But it is a two-edged sword, and the balance is delicate between its being an advantage and a burden.

It is important for young achievers to recognize the need

for greater sensitivity to those who are older and those who have achieved less. This need becomes basic as more and more young executives find themselves managing more experienced older subordinates at all levels in all professions. The smart young success (and, for that matter, any young person finding himself or herself in a similar situation) realizes that he or she is operating in what subordinates often see as a crisis situation. Communication becomes crucial. Reassurances must be given.

The burden of the responsibility for both falls, always, squarely on the shoulders of the young executive/lawyer/editor /administrator. These people are expected to possess wisdom far beyond their years, not only in business decisions but in interpersonal relations. Often the obtaining of such wisdom begins with the learning of a whole new language. A 31-year-old marketing analyst and a 50-year-old marketing analyst may not speak the same tongue, or, if they do, then the vocabulary is often radically different. But it is the younger who must adapt to make the elder feel more comfortable. Success only intensifies the depth of the generation gap.

Most of the young successes had techniques for dealing with the problem. Ira Lipman, like many of those interviewed, goes out of his way to talk to older employees, question them about how things are going, listen to their opinions and advice. That doesn't necessarily mean that the advice is always taken. Listening with respect, even though you're the boss, is important in personnel relations. From listening and trying to grasp the personal dynamics of the situation, young successes developed great sensitivity to older workers. Much of that sensitivity was rooted in childhood, in the common ability to be comfortable with adults and be able to learn from them.

In some cases, the sensitivity was born of being on the receiving end of age prejudice. Norman Spaulding jumped ship to another company when Mattel turned him down for an important district manager's spot on the basis he was "too young for such a mature position." Other achievers mention—some with bitterness—being passed over or not considered at all because of their age. Such failures—and as a group the achievers had many of them, being inherent risk-takers—abounded and gave them a certain depth of feeling about relations with coworkers.

Young managers, bank presidents, professors, editors and entrepreneurs are already extremely conscious of their age and relative lack of experience. They are aware of it within their immediate circle of business. But the pressure to prove increases when said young achiever is dealing professionally with those out of the home office. Ross Johnson was a young-looking 45 when he took the helm at Standard Brands in 1976. A stockholder in her sixties took one look at his picture in the annual report and wrote the company that she was selling her shares. While such blatant instances of mistrust of youth and a young appearance are becoming increasingly rare as youth shows its corporate stuff, there is still a significant residue with which a young success must deal, and handle with tact and care. Lehman Brothers partner Steven Fenster, 34, has been described as the single best known banker under 40 on Wall Street. Although in investment banking much of the innovative thinking and sheer energy comes from the young, the leadership comes from those older, and Fenster can see the sense of it:

> Every time we're dealing with someone important the great client relation problem is that we're interacting with people who are older. The way we handle it is to have a limited number of "old" people involved in the process. Clients are very reassured by their participation in the relationship. It's critical that the client recognize that a lot of the substantive thinking is done by me. But the client has to think that someone like Pete Peterson or George Ball is sufficiently on top of it. Heads of corporations need reassurance from people close to their age even though they know that maybe the intellectual work has been done on a different level.

The need for such reassurance is not the exclusive property of Wall Street. It reaches into the boardroom as well. Even if a man or woman has become very successful while young, cosmetics may sometimes count more than corporate savvy. Ann Leven became treasurer of the Metropolitan Museum of Art in New York at age 32. Today, at 39, she looks ten years younger. Like other early achievers, she notices that headhunters seeking people for corporate boards find a resistance by those boards if the candidate looks young. Leven recalls overhearing a conversation between two foundation officers who were considering her for membership on their board. The officers noted that when she looked a little older she would be fine. Leven and others are convinced that appearance, superficial as it may seem, can be an important factor in such selections. Having a few strands of gray hair can sometimes be a boon to furthering the young achiever's career, ironically at the same time as much older executives with a youthful appearance are prized for their ability to stay looking young. Looking the part may not be so crucial as it was in the past, but it is still a consideration.

All this comes in the light of proof that doubts about youth in power are fading away. During the last four years, directors at more than twelve large companies have tapped new chief executive officers in their thirties and forties. In a survey conducted by Forbes of the 200 highest paid corporation chiefs, one in twelve now in office got his job by the age of 40. Although this can be encouraging to early achievers, and those who aspire to become same, there remains the unchanging problem of the constant pressure to pack a lifetime of experience into a short span of time. As technology and communication become more sophisticated, the fast track can get only faster. Most of the young successes interviewed have been able to pack in the experience needed and the technological expertise where it applies. But they realize that a certain amount of inevitable business and personal catch-up must be played. They experience a gap between age and acumen. Because early bloomers are young, after all, regardless of smarts and drive, they can make mistakes. And their mistakes are ten times more visible from the start because of their position and relative youth.

Such mistakes can often form a predictable pattern. During the last twenty years, industrial psychologist William B. Plasse worked with more than a dozen top young industrial and business executives. He lists the following as the most common mistakes inherent in those he has studied, and they neatly fit those of the young success breed as well.

1. Regardless of a young boss's talents and intuitions, he or she lacks the experience and exposure that only can come with age. Couple that with an impatient nature, which is quickly dissatisfied if things and people don't advance as quickly as the achiever does, and you have a classic case of wanting too much too fast. This could have negative implications if the young executive makes acquisitions without thoroughly examining the implications of corporate or personal expansion.

2. The business and personal philosophy of young executives is in many cases relatively undeveloped. Often such people don't know if they're in business to make money, build a monument or just have fun. Without these values clearly defined, such achievers many times have little to fall back on when the going gets rough.

3. The reconciliation of theory and practice hasn't had time to develop in the younger executive. Perhaps a young turk will do things by the book, trying to acquire the people management skills that executives three times his age have been developing for years. Part of this problem could be attributed to the lack of people-oriented courses in business schools. There is no teacher like experience, and often it is difficult

for a young boss to make the transition from being an individual shining star to becoming the top member of a team that must be carefully, delicately and decisively guided.

4. The need to learn the hard way is a maninfestation of that old need by achievers to be independent and different. Many young successful executives are extremely self-critical. They have a tendency to blame themselves if something goes wrong. It is difficult for anyone to strike the fragile balance between being an all-knowing corporate leader on one hand and on the other, an eager learner who listens to the advice of subordinates and coworkers who have been at the company for many years. When to take advice and when to discard it is an important lesson that one must learn through trial and error. A young executive *must* learn faster than most. Often errors can't afford to be made, for a young success is in a very visible position.

5. Simply because they are young, such achievers tend to misjudge their own abilities. They haven't been around long enough to know. In their special areas they might overrate their abilities and talents. On the other hand, they can sabotage themselves in those areas where they see themselves as weak. Their tendency is to come down hard when they make a mistake, to be too critical of themselves, assuming responsibility and sometimes guilt for things that would be better kept in perspective.

6. Young executives sometimes don't take enough time to think. Because they are so driven, they dive right in and consequently have trouble establishing and maintainning priorities. When one is impatient, everything is immediate. There could be a tendency to be enchanted with something today and to forget about it tomorrow. Sometimes impatience and drive sabotage necessary follow-through and planning.

Although Plasse is not specifically talking about young successes, he could be. Obviously, if a young success made all the aforementioned mistakes to great degree and often, he or she wouldn't be a young success. But the pattern is there, and it is the smart achiever who can recognize potential mistakes and deal with them quickly and with perspective.

Sometimes people are successful not in spite of their failures, but because of them. Failure is an important element in any success. From failure one grows, learns, expands. The failure to get the desired promotion could be the necessary jolt one needs to try for another job or another company. Mistakes for young successes must be made, and while they become much more visible because of the relative youth and position of the individual, they are an essential part of the growing process. The successes talk of their many failures—the presence of failure also implies the courage to risk and win—in positive terms, in terms of what was learned, accomplished because of such setbacks. This is another element that separates the superachiever from the mainstream. It is often tempting to quit after a frustration, to remain where one is because the setback has drained one of confidence and zest. But those who see the wall ahead and try to figure out a way to get over or around it, those who plunge in, anyway, are those who win. Failure is never pleasant, but if you let it stop you altogether, you will never know success. That message is strong with those who become successful young. They are just as hurt by failure as the rest of us. But they didn't let failure stop them. In business, mistakes that are made in the name of youth or ambition are sometimes major but never fatal. They are instead necessary to the process.

———

A young achiever has his or her work cut out at the office: there's sniping by subordinates and superiors, mistrust by outside business contacts and the pressure of having to handle problems with the wisdom and tact of someone twenty years older. But the dark patterns do not stop there. If anything, they are more intense in a young achiever's personal life. In talks with young successes, there is a defensive, almost apologetic, attitude about making it quickly. No one better realizes in what an uncomfortable role he or she has put others than the young achiever. All around are people who have worked hard for many years to get where the achiever got in a very few. Such realizations are not lost on those who get to the top young. Indeed, their sensitivity to those older is one reason they were able to attain their goal in the first place. But the end result of such sensitivity is often a bending over backwards to minimize the achievement the individual has worked so hard to attain. While there are exceptions, most of the young successes interviewed spoke of frequently and consciously downplaying their position to make others feel more comfortable.

Sometimes this downplaying takes on the guise of refusing to recognize, at least publicly, that one is successful. Jane Pauley was 26 when she was selected to be Barbara Walters' successor on the "Today" show on NBC. At the time of her appointment, it was apparent that few broadcast journalists had won national recognition as quickly as Pauley, who only five years earlier had been a senior at Indiana University. Although she competed with many qualified professional women much older than she, and won hands-down in the interview, viewer response and poise categories, she finds it hard to believe that it happened. She has said that her age was her chief liability, and is sometimes uncomfortable with the notion of being called successful. One of the highest paid and most visible women in the nation, Pauley nevertheless would not be interviewed for this book. Not because she was uncomfortable with interviews, but because, in her words, "I don't consider myself successful. I'm really not the sort of person who should be in a book like this." Yet she is, and fits in perfectly, although in interviews she still takes great pains

to point out that she knows she is young and is fully prepared
to go back to general-assignment reporting in Indianapolis,
should she wake up and find out the "Today" show job was just
a dream.

Succeeding young can be a difficult situation for anyone.
Contemporaries aren't on the early success level of achievement.
Childhood and college friends are quickly outgrown. Older business peers at the same time don't share many of the "young"
social mores and activities that the younger generation does. As
a result, most of the achievers interviewed opted to socialize with
their contemporaries, while at the same time consciously mini-
mizing their accomplishments in order to keep the social lines
of communication open.

Young successes downplay in many ways. The "what-do-you-
do" business trip conversation can become an ordeal. At 25,
Jane Evans gained national attention as the president of I. Miller.
In that capacity, the bright young business graduate had
to travel frequently. Inevitably the person seated next to her on
the plane was an older man who would ask her what she did
for a living. She says she "was almost embarrassed frankly to tell
them what I did. I'd be on an airplane and the people would
say, 'oh, you're a stewardess,' and I'd say, 'No,' and they'd say,
'What business are you in,' and I'd say, 'The fashion business,'
and I'd do everything not to tell them until they'd finally say,
'What's your title,' and I'd say in a small voice, 'I'm the president.' I'd feel sorry for the Willy Loman types when I told
them what I did. Often they'd say, 'Are you a buyer?' and I'd
just say, 'Yes'."

For some successes the downplaying is a simple matter of
sensitivity to the feelings of others. For other achievers, it
is a matter of self-defense, a self-effacement needed to insure
smoother working conditions. When Lucinda Franks won the
Pulitzer Prize, she had to learn that defense. Like other achievers, she learned when to use it as an offense, too. Her coworkers,

particularly the men who had been working on her newspaper for many years, were hostile and jealous. Eventually she developed a "sense of guilt about these old people who have worked for so long. I got a little embarrassed by it. Now I seldom tell people I've won the Pulitzer—I'll tell someone every once in a while if there's a graceful way to do it. Or in a situation where older, particularly male journalists look at me and say, 'Oh, what a cute nice girl. Do you work in the research department?' And I'll play them along for a while and then just drop it in and watch the shock register."

One of the advantages of being successful young is that when people assume a young man or woman is in a lackey-type position by dint of age alone and assume so in a manner that is condescending, the achiever can play his or her trump card to deflate pompous egos. The shock value of a baby-faced upstart announcing he is president of a $100-million company can't be underestimated. Many mentioned playing such a hand with glee —but only on rare occasions.

The same drive, intelligence and impatience that marks the rise to the top can also mark a quick outgrowing of friends. Most people cannot keep pace with the interests, the perpetual motion of an early achiever, and this creates stress for the achiever and those around him or her. Men who are early achievers often date older women because most of the young women in their peer group have neither the business acumen nor the broad horizons of success orientation that they do. Women achievers often date older men for the same reasons. The older date or wife or husband often functions as a bridge between older business peers and a stable private life with contemporaries. Of those young achievers interviewed who are married, most were married to spouses at least three and as many as fifteen years older than they. While there are exceptions—men marrying peer group women or younger, those individuals who have kept a few close friends from school days to present—most recall with bittersweetness the frequent surpassing of friends. Entrepreneur Steven Markoff muses that friends "understand but they don't understand. They come over to the house and blame their uncomfortableness on my having money, but what they're really saying, I think, is that they just don't understand what is missing in them. 'What cube of uranium am I missing that generates all this power? Where does it all come from?' They tell you you should be happy, that you're successful and have two cars and if they had two cars they would be eternally happy. And you want to grab them by the throat and say, 'You stupid son of a bitch, don't you understand?' "

Such statements, echoed by many of the achievers interviewed, bring up the question as to whether or not the attainment of early success is good for one's psyche. Certainly, those who have made it to the top young have done so because they are able to deal with the professional and personal problems that such a position brings. They could handle the jealousy, envy, hostility and fawning, they could dodge the swipes by those hoping to bring them down, those waiting to capitalize on the least mistake. But once there, and there so fast, a peculiar feeling of self-doubt arises in most of them, and they question if everything has come too fast, too soon.

In what could be a form of downplaying, many of the young successes sense that accomplishing before they feel they deserve to accomplish can bring big problems. Lucinda Franks "went into a kind of depression" after she won the Pulitzer, and she took a leave of absence from work for nearly two years. During that time she was supposed to be writing a book, but "Mainly, I just vegetated. I had seen so many other people who did stories that were just as good or even better than mine, and I guess I didn't believe that I was 'that' good. I think it's dangerous to get such an award when you're young."

For Steven Markoff, friends—not an award—touched off the doubts:

> People say, "You're holding out the truth from us." Well, the answer is that when you are prospecting in the world, looking for that rainbow, the worst thing you can do is find that rainbow, find the pot of gold. What are you going to do with the pot of gold? Say, "Look, go bury it again and I'll start looking"? That is the problem. I don't have a solution.

R. Stephen Lefler found that his early corporate success at DesignResearch created a social void at work:

> You find you don't have that many close friends. One of the problems in reaching a senior position is that of detachment. There's no longer the camaraderie of the buddies in the office who drink and raise hell and do a good job. But let me tell you what's really tough. All your life you perform and suddenly you're at the top. Mentally it's rough. There's nobody to pat you on the back. That's the biggest surprise. All your life you're geared for a day-to-day struggle and then you come to a situation where that struggle comes every month at a board meeting . . . I should have board meetings every two weeks, instead.

Many of the young successes were somewhat in awe of what they had accomplished. They were in a strange state of suspension, not really able to believe it all. It was as if there existed an "evil eye" mentality, which said that if you admit your success, such success will go away. While again there are exceptions—those who worked hard for what they had and felt that that work justified a quick rise and the attendant power—the majority to one degree or another did not feel quite "arrived." This, of course, did not stop them from continuing to achieve, from being capable and innovative and using all those things they possessed in order to become successful. But the awesomeness of it all comes to the forefront from time to time in most cases. For Lee Eisenberg, one particular situation gave cause for shudders:

> It's staggering to me because my eyes see the same thing and I'm looking at the world as though I never got out of eighth grade—only now we have a lot of expensive toys to play with. I would go off to a writers conference at a college and sit down on the floor of an English professor's house with a gallon of hearty burgundy and these students would sit down at my feet and ask the most reverential kinds of questions. I just wanted to scream and get the hell out of there. How could they possibly do that to me? I don't look like that, do I?

Such uncomfortableness, such pleas for understanding and such gaps in achievement vis-à-vis age are inherent in young successes. No matter how accomplished, how self-confident, how capable the individual, there will always be such reactions. Our society is not entirely geared to having power in the hands of the young. When young people do achieve powerful positions —as they are doing in increasing numbers—they are not always fully able to enjoy all the psychological and societal fruits of their labors. They must be sensitive to those who did not achieve, must be careful with their friends, must bridge large maturity gulfs daily, must speak their own as well as the language of their older coworkers, must live with the knowledge that their mistakes are ten times more visible than those of their older coworkers. They may have estates, expensive cars and clothes and zippy vacations, but they tend not to flaunt. For young achievers are in some ways victims of a double success standard. They are cautious, feeling—rightly or wrongly—that society is uncomfortable with young cigar-chomping tycoons.

That's a demanding package to shoulder, but why should those who are not superachievers be particularly sympathetic? Because the average achiever has more in common with the young success than he or she realizes. The problems of early accomplishment—holding on to a sense of self, the need to value one's abilities in perspective, the hurt of outgrowing friends, the sting of failure, the fear of risk, the painful visibility of mistakes and the need to be particularly sensitive to others who might threaten or be threatened in some way—are problems with which we each must deal, to some degree, throughout our lives.

The way in which a young success handles these delicate personal and professional pitfalls will mark the difference between ultimate success and failure. It is crucial to temper cockiness with tact, the desire to talk with the desire to listen, isolation with communication. The key is growth. If one can learn from the inevitable mistakes and failures which happen to each of us, one is on the right success track, even if other "success" traits might not seem to apply.

The ability to be flexible, perceptive and sensitive to the needs and fears of others is present in each of us. It's simply exercised more by some than by others. If young successes seem different, it is perhaps because they have been able to look upon even the negative side of achievement as a challenge. This willingness to conquer an obstacle is one trait which makes them winners.

# 5 ▤ The Corporate Squeeze Play

WE OFTEN LOOK with a certain smugness at those who made it at an early age. We think that if someone has had a meteoric rise, then it only stands to reason he or she will have a meteoric decline. The parable of the tortoise and the hare is a comforting one: the quick, flash-in-the-pans might seem to be winning the race at first, but we know—tradition tells us—that the slow and steady will inherit the earth. In many instances, of course, that is true. Whatever happened to the inventor of the hula hoop? Remember the Pet Rock? Fads like those and the people who spearhead them are by nature short-lived. The inventors and businesspeople behind such fads recognize that and even plan for obsolescence . . . while laughing all the way to the bank.

But building a career is a different thing, and young achievers are a different breed. Unlike a hula-hoop marketer, achievers plan to be around for quite a while. They plan to be achieving as much as they can for the long term. They are the hares in the

race, certainly. But they have the shrewdness and solidity of the
tortoise, too. In effect they are running their own race, and often
start before the rest of the field has its shoes laced up. Because
that inner race is an intense one, the chances for mistakes are by
nature greater. But so are the chances for reward. This risk factor,
as we have seen, is built into an achiever's constitution.

With the attendant problems of holding a responsible position at a young age, it would seem that if the achievers do not
actually burn out fast, then they would at least worry about it constantly. Surprisingly, the "early ripe-early rot" syndrome is not so
strong in these people as we would initially suspect. Why? Simply because they are so inherently restless that it is not in their
makeup to stay in one place or profession long enough to
burn out.

Most early achievers instinctively follow the advice of Frank
L. Carney, who at age 39 can today look back on a solid and
lucrative business career spanning twenty years. At age 19, he co-
founded the Pizza Hut restaurant chain, and quickly found
himself a wealthy man. Carney says with modesty that he "just
happens" to be where he is, as if his years of hard work and sharp
inbred business sense were a fluke. But one of the reasons he
"happens" to be a sustained young success story is that he didn't
relish any attained goal for very long. He didn't sit on his laurels,
but instead enjoyed them briefly and then refocused his efforts
on another goal. He did this, he says, because he needed to have
something to look forward to. Just as we look forward to the next
promotion, so young successes look forward to the next success
and challenge leading to that success. Carney's attitude is typical
of early achievers, who frequently talk about what job they
would like to do next while barely ensconced in their present
position. They often stress that the job they are in is not the
place where they will spend the rest of their lives.

How much of this is a solid and conscious business strategy
and how much is a needed defense against personal fears of peak-

ing early is hard to ascertain. There is a little of both in each achiever. But the fact remains that being successful young has one strong advantage: when the job gets boring, one is still young enough to move on to another job or even another profession. Sense of self gives young successes a grounding and at the same time shoves them along. Sometimes, it shoves them too fast. There is a strong hint of needing to move quickly before even the thought of burning out could have a chance to hit.

This one-step-ahead-of-the-sheriff mentality is the opposite side of the coin from the tortoise mentality, which so often dogs the average achiever. If young successes frequently err on the side of restlessness, then average achievers frequently wait too long for things to come to them. The happy medium, the ideal mix of judgment and impulse, comes not with age, but with the ability to know when restlessness can work and when it can hinder. It is interesting to note, however, that restlessness in general seems to have served the young achievers well. If the hare is quick to run a race and loses, he is still more energetic than the tortoise and thereby is able to run more races. When one runs more races than the competition, the odds of winning— or at least finishing in the money—are greatly improved.

That's not to say that all young successes are comfortable about their current positions. Stephen Lefler muses about the day when the novelty of his youth wears off, when he's 40 and "it's not going to be a big deal to be president of a half-billion dollar company at forty." Already solidly in a second career at an age when most are starting out on their first, David Obst has considered the problem on a different plane:

> Whenever you get up too high you're going to come down. Highs and lows are compounded if you're younger because, though outwardly you have the confidence, inwardly all young people who become successful are not sure if it's real or not. And the reason they're not sure is because they're still young

and successful and have their whole future ahead of them. There are so many flashes in the pan today. The media burns out public figures so quickly, and once you've had the slightest touch of public adulation and coverage it's a narcotic. You become addicted to it.

Enormous insecurities develop which drive a person that much harder to be successful and it becomes a cyclical thing of: "Nothing's happening, I have to make it keep happening so I can become successful." Young successful people don't have the perspective to sit and enjoy success while it's happening. They're driven by the need to get high again. The great tragedy comes when the people begin to believe their own myths and their own infallibility. You stop listening to people who are older. It's the worst mistake young successful people make. You start to take yourself too seriously. Yet underneath it all you still have the person who believes it's all going to be taken away and that it was due to flukes. Even in the most successful of people, it's never resolved.

Jann Wenner is a controversial and flamboyant young success whose idiosyncrasies can be explained in the light of Obst's comments on achiever insecurity. Wenner was an unknown ten years ago: unemployed, nearly broke, he had dropped out of the University of California at Berkeley. His future seemed dim. But Wenner possessed the traits that mark all young achievers from an early age: he was hyperenergetic, extremely restless, driven, determined, ambitious, brimming with ideas. He was also very much a loner. His businessman father (who described his son as "a pain in the ass, but we knew he would make something of himself") and his mother divorced when he was young. As a result, Wenner was shipped off to boarding school in Southern California. This early trauma, an isolation from his family, contributed to his own isolation. While initially painful, it also proved a fertile spawning ground for his ambition.

In 1967, Wenner persuaded relatives and friends to put up $7,500 so he could start a new magazine devoted to the pop culture of his Sixties generation. Possessed of the young success trait of compatibility with adults, as well as a great deal of personal charm, he persuaded a printer to provide him with credit and free office space and cajoled a staff to work gratis as well. Thus was *Rolling Stone* born, and within ten years it grew into a lucrative national magazine that came to symbolize the changing social consciousness of a generation, while at the same time providing an exciting showcase for solid, yet unknown writing talent. Wenner was hailed as a wunderkind, a publishing genius along the lines of a William Randolph Hearst or Henry Luce. And he played the part: a lavish mansion in San Francisco was home and the scene of the best parties; he was seen in all the right places with the right celebrities. Jann Wenner had it made, and made it fast.

But Wenner also had some personal and business failures within his success. An abrasive, hot-and-cold personality left him open to swipes from friends and associates. His critics said he often acted on impulse in business decisions and therefore lost great amounts of money. His penchant for being the only one in charge was so strong that frequent firings were the norm. The masthead of the magazine seemed to turn over every few months. He spent money on publishing books that were never properly marketed, on prototypes of magazines that never got out of the starting gate. *Rolling Stone* remained successful and gained important readership, but Wenner's other ventures were less satisfying. Staffers noticed that he was beginning to believe his own press, and often modestly referred to himself as a wunderkind. Early success for Wenner was inevitable, but created many deep conflicts. He would not be interviewed because he is reluctant to talk about himself. He fiercely protects his privacy and seemingly can't let his guard down. In an interview with *New Times* magazine, a close Wenner associate summed up the fear that Wenner personifies. This is a fear that all young successes feel —to greater or lesser degree—at some point in their lives:

Jann has never gotten over the suspicion that maybe he just lucked into his success, just happened to be the right man at the right time with exactly the right idea. And that everything just worked, not because of what he did, but because of the times we were in. That's why he never stops pushing. It's something that happens to a lot of guys who find success at an early age. Okay, you've made it once—so what's your next trick? That's the question that keeps staring Jann in the face.

Wenner is not alone. The fear of failure, of growing old, of what-will-I-do-next is a strong deterrent to moving ahead for each of us, achiever and non-achiever alike. This fear becomes more intense the more successful one is. If you've been the editor of a national magazine at 29, where do you go from there? What new horizons are left if you're president of a bank at 31, or the head of the university at 28? If Wenner realizes that such a drive/self-destruct mechanism exists in his makeup, he hasn't said so publicly. But other young successes have. They recognize in themselves the insecurity that Obst discusses and Wenner seems to live. Each of them possesses it somehow, and most openly acknowledge it is there. Most also go one step further and try to deal with it via introspection, the help of friends or, in rare cases, with professional help. The candor that marks these achievers comes from a highly developed sense of self, and helps them to deal with the infinite complications of achievement— including insecurity.

It's not in the nature of young successes to stay in one place for long. New horizons must be found. Some search desperately, making the inevitable mistakes anyone makes when things are not thought through. In doing that, others suffer, too. Perhaps staffs are hired for a new magazine that can't possibly get off the ground. Because of inadequate research, these people are soon out of a job. A new company folds within months of its inception—for the same reason—and others are left out in the cold.

But such a desperate search on the part of young achievers is

an exception. The rule is quite different. Many have set out sys-
tematically, evaluating where they are, where they have been and
where they want to go. For some, new horizons are found by
changing to a different field. If you're at the top of yours in your
late 20s, the challenge of a new area of endeavor is particularly
inviting. Like climbing Mt. Everest because "it's there," a young
success is inspired by that which is new. Joe Armstrong went
from being a Wall Street lawyer to publisher. Leon Botstein gave
up two promising careers as a professional musician, conductor
and a serious scholar—to pursue the equally arduous path of university administrator.

For others, new challenges are found by supplementing success
with outside projects. Secure in his business, Steven Markoff
takes exotic trips and tries adventurous sports like skydiving and
hot-air ballooning. Alan Dershowitz writes for national magazines
and has a full-time thriving law practice on the side in addition
to his Harvard professorship. Ira Lipman founded the Tennessee
Young Republican Party and is active in politics in his home
state. Bank president Lynn Salvage is a member of the board
of directors for civic and business groups. Other young successes race cars, belong to boards of directors of corporations or
educational institutions, write novels, conduct seminars. The
horizon always moves a bit further away each time; the young
success does not know when to stop. The biggest challenge of all,
for achievers and non-achievers alike, is in recognizing insecurities
and conquering them before proceeding. Then the other worlds
are easier and the concept of "burning out" young remains just
that— a concept.

Not all young successes sustain, of course. The logs of business, academia, finance, law and publishing are jammed with
those who flashed and were heard from no more. Those fast-
track people who quickly reach the limits of their abilities and
stop will always be with us. But young successes as a breed have
extra dimensions that give them staying power. Some might

point to the Wall Street whizz kids of the go-go Sixties as a perfect example of quick achievement–quick decline. The group of them, much-publicized for their youth, risk-taking capability and affluence, seem to be all but gone. Stories abound: some ended up selling pretzels on street corners when the market turned bearish; one young star turned to raising Irish setters in a New York City loft.

But the majority of those whizzkids returned to the Street— or never left it—continuing in the always-risky business of dealing with other people's money. If many of them are not perceived as geniuses now, it is because the nature of their business has changed: the dizzying conditions that made overnight million-aires of them simply do not exist. The "glamour" is gone. Pos-sessed of the young success traits that separate them from the mainstream, many of those Wall Street geniuses did bounce back. And they bounced back because they were flexible, aware, ever-ambitious. The spark did not die simply because the glow was gone; they kept moving to the next challenge. And most of them continue to produce—and succeed—far beyond the abilities of anyone we might term "burnt out."

Take the case of Jerry Tsai. He personified Wall Street's glamour years. At 30, he became nationally known as an accurate, high-rolling trader of growth companies. Growth was his most important product. His reading of the market—which stocks were hot, which would rise and which would become tomorrow's leftovers—became legendary. The press covered his rise: born in Shanghai, he came to America when he was 17, graduated from Boston University with a degree in economics. At the age of 29, he started Fidelity Capital, a pioneering public growth fund—the forerunner to today's performance funds. His reputation as a genius was quickly established.

In 1965, Tsai struck out on his own and formed the Manhat-tan Fund. Expecting to sell $25 million in shares, he instead sold

$270 million, relying on old standby glamour stocks like Xerox, IBM and Polaroid. But by 1967 the glamour stocks had become overpriced, and Tsai was too busy to recognize what was happening. The stocks didn't move and Tsai, by nature a trader, needed to instead be an investor. The market went down: Tsai's fund suffered.

But Tsai wasn't finished. Today, if not glamorous, then he is at least once again successful. And in a big way: he sold his management corporation to a large insurance holding company, and holds stock in it worth about $35 million. He has embarked on a new career in developing noninsurance acquisitions for his new company: mutual funds, personal loans, construction, hotels. His sense of growth is today paying off, but in a different way. He's not speculating, but building.

Tsai typifies those who have had a great success while young. It is often difficult to keep at the same level of achievement throughout one's life. To an achiever, not accomplishing anything new and wonderful is often the same thing as having had a failure. It is difficult to find new challenges that will meet the time and energy requirements of a young charger; constructive opportunities for growth narrow as one gets to the top. But young successes, those who truly fit the definition, are not flashes in the pan. They are possessed of a solidity that can ride out fame, and learn from it.

═══

If being successful young brings with it a plethora of professional and business adjustments, then being young, successful and a woman ups that ante considerably. While society is changing to accept young people in power and is also changing its view of a woman's place in that power structure, the changes are not as swift in coming as both groups would like. Today being a successful woman is hard enough, but being a young woman in a position of power brings a deluge of difficulties. Jane Evans had a taste of some of them when she left the presidency of I. Miller to assume the duties of vice president for Butterick Fashion Marketing:

> Being a woman is a double whammy—good or bad, depending on how the observer chooses to look at it. It's a tremendous advantage being young and being female but at the same time you have to prove a lot more than you would ordinarily have to prove. When they [the employees] first heard I was a female, that was bad enough. But when they heard I was 30, they voted to have mass resignations. They were just not going to put up with it.

Evans' staff did not resign, of course. But like any young woman in business, she was and is faced with many misconceptions. People will say a woman got her job only because of affirmative action, under threat of lawsuits (minorities have to labor under this calumny as well). She will be the recipient of a hundred tiny tests from older male counterparts, subordinates and superiors as well as older women subordinates, to prove she is worthy of the job. These tests come with the territory, and smart businesswomen are aware they will have to face such trials. Smart businesswomen have also learned to ignore the she-got-there-because-she-slept-with-the-boss syndrome. But it is harder to ignore those tests that come from her male contemporaries, who perceive a compounded threat to their position and ego. Ford Foundation management specialist Robert Schrank sees the situation as a giant squeeze play: since organizations usually have a pyramidal structure, the process of moving up the corporate ladder into the higher reaches of the pyramid automatically involves squeezing someone out of the running. As women climb the power ladder, men are doubly threatened because the number of pyramid squeeze players is increasing, and their masculinity is on the block. Because such women are young, they will be competing for a long time. Add to that pressure the reality of a shrunken job market, and women achievers find themselves facing the proverbial double bind.

It is not our purpose to detail the problems women have traditionally had and will have in business until that elusive and constantly changing goal of equality is reached. Much has been written elsewhere on that subject. But it is important to consider the young success effects on female achievers. Entry into business was in many cases easier for the baby boomers than for their older sisters. The Vietnam war provided increased opportunities that would normally have been taken by the many young men who were fighting, protesting, studying or evading. Affirmative action, backed up by lawsuits and a budding women's movement, boosted the number of professional avenues women could take. But along with the boost came an escalation of problems. When *Business Week* listed the top one hundred corporate women in 1976, almost all of them refused to disclose their age. Some might attribute this to female vanity, but it could also be interpreted as a defense. Most of the women pictured appeared to be under forty. Many of them had probably felt the criticism—and skepticism—that greets a young achiever, and were trying to head it off.

Whether many of these corporate women, including the young successful women interviewed, would have made it to the top anyway without benefit of movements and lawsuits is of course debatable. The achieving male or female possesses qualities that will pull him or her through in the most difficult of times and against stiff odds. Achievers will rise to the top when others will only throw up their hands in exasperation. But it is undeniable that one of the effects of affirmative action has been to give more women an opportunity to seize power, and that opportunity is coming younger. With it came the problems that the achiever of today has already faced, and is facing still.

Author and management expert Caroline Bird observes that youth is less of a barrier to women than men, while age is more a barrier to a woman than a man. Women, Bird says, are still forced to prove themselves better, and sooner, than their male contemporaries.

When a woman does prove she is equal to the task, she might find the top of the pyramid a lonely place, for sexism can be practiced by women as well as men. Often the woman who has been at the company for a long time and who has not advanced will find it hard to understand a younger female coming in over her. The woman achiever finds herself resented, not only by older men and men her age, but by older women. To make it young only intensifies such resentment. Bank president Lynn Salvage has seen that happen, and understands why:

> The one thing that bothers me is the allegation that I progressed because I was a woman. There is still some truth to the fact that you have to be very, very good as a woman in order to achieve. There is an advantage in being young in the confidence factor. Many of the women who have been in the business community, say, for twenty years longer than I have, have been sort of stifled and stepped upon and in many ways what I call broken. So they never really achieved the level of confidence they should have had. Young women do have more confidence than their older counterparts because they haven't had the many years of conditioning that they are second-class citizens.

But there are some signs that such resentment of women by other women is lessening. While they do face envy and the problems that have dogged women in the business world, young females entering the power structure today have a bit more going for them than their older professional sisters. The "second-class citizen" feeling, so often borne in silence by older women in business, is absent. The baby-boom woman has received the benefit of a heightened awareness and new avenues of opportunity unequaled for women in the history of this country. And as the younger woman realizes her power, she is able to share it a little. The "old boy" crony network modus operandi is being adopted by women in business. They're not hoarding those ideas they'll never use, those opportunities they don't want anyway. They're not falling for the old divide-and-conquer trick of never trusting another female. Now women in business are beginning to share, to build a network of opportunity and advice all their own. While women still have a long way to go before achieving positional and monetary equality with men (indeed, some say such equality won't be reached until the day mediocre women are promoted just as mediocre men have been) the emergence of the "new girl network" makes it easier to deal with the professional and personal problems that arise for women aiming at the top of the business ladder.

Many of these problems are self-inflicted. Now that women have been active in the executive workforce for a measurable stretch of time, new studies are coming to light about their reactions to business situations. Simmons College management professors Margaret Hennig and Anne Jardim, trailblazers in the study of women and the effects of women on business and vice versa, describe areas in which a woman in business is unintentionally likely to do herself in. Hennig/Jardim say that women in business often describe themselves as waiting to be chosen for a promotion, hesitant to take the initiative and having a tendency to wait to be told what to do. The same women describe themselves as feeling confused and conflicted about their goals, and reluctant to take risk. The feelings of guilt over having a career, so easily dispelled intellectually but so difficult to eliminate emotionally, are strong, and frequently women try to make up for them by becoming the perfect woman or mother or wife—an impossible situation in which something has got to give.

Young achieving women, however, seem to avoid many of

the pitfalls of their less accomplished sisters. Because perhaps they have associated with those who are older and gleaned from them valuable advice and guidance, the successful women interviewed did not mention an unusual amount of resentment or sexism on the part of their colleagues who were older women. They did experience the same problems (somewhat compounded) with older male superiors and coworkers, as well as their male contemporaries, but did not mention resentment to any extraordinary degree in women their age who are also in business. If anything, these women make it a point to eagerly share opportunities, gossip, job openings and professional advice with each other and subordinates.

Contrary to the Hennig/Jardim "trap" list, young achieving women instinctively go out after a promotion, barging in with the traditional male "play me or trade me" attitude. They take the initiative, creating projects that show them in the best light and consequently they generate more opportunities. They work toward an immediate and specified goal. They don't wait to be told what to do. The element of risk-taking comes with the breed.

On a personal front, young successful women do feel that societal guilt about not spending all day at home tending the hearth. But they deal with it in different ways. Many of the women interviewed were strongly defensive about questions pertaining to their social life and family—how could they possibly keep it all together and hold a responsible job, too?—but they were at the same time candid about their feelings of trying to do too much, of the "freak" positions that many of them had been put in. Pulitzer Prize winner Lucinda Franks remembers an early time when she did not quite fit in:

> I walked into the London office of United Press International the exact moment they were being delivered a suit by the British Civil Liberties Union for having no women in all of Asia, Europe and Africa. They became very excited that they

could hire a "hungry" young woman for slave wages. That's essentially how I got my job there. Women, when they enter a "male" profession, have to work twice as hard. It's like a Black going into a redneck town in the deep South trying to sell something. The horrible thing about it is that in the whole process of cracking that male world and winning in that male world you distort. You're forced to deny your own femininity. I never wore a dress. The greatest triumph I had was one day when one of my editors looked up at me and said, "'You know something, I don't think of you as a woman any more. You're a journalist." My heart swelled. That was the highest compliment he could give me.

The candor of young female—and male—achievers comes with years of business seasoning jammed into a short period of time. Young women achievers have been sniped at, viewed with suspicion and tested tenfold by all around them. They emerge from such trials with a strong definition of self, feelings of self-worth and self-defense far beyond their years. Even Jane Pauley, who didn't consider herself particularly "successful," nevertheless showed that success presence in an interview shortly after assuming the "Today" post:

> I think I've performed competently enough. There are a lot of women in the position where people say, "She does it so well, for her age," because doors started opening to them not too many years ago. I'd rather endure those remarks and still have a very good opportunity than not have it at all.

Women achievers see the business and personal double standard, and try to tackle it with the same energy that they tackle a business problem. They are beginning to deal with it by being themselves, not someone's timeworn image of the business-woman-as-bespectacled-matron-in-sensible-shoes. That image is fading along with that of the spinster schoolmarm.

Joyce Hughes rejected those images a long time ago. The

first Black woman to join the faculty of the University of Minnesota Law School, she was also the first female clerk for a federal judge in Minnesota:

> A person's individual success depends on her definition of herself. Being a Black woman means society defines me negatively—I reject that definition. In rejecting a definition that society imposes on you, you are motivated to prove the validity of the definition you choose. I am a strong believer in self as a motivating force. If you want to be successful, you have to discipline yourself to make hard choices.

Young achieving women like Hughes, who currently teaches at Northwestern University, reject stereotypes while accepting leadership, creating opportunities for it whenever possible just as their male counterparts do. These women have learned to delegate authority, to have a sensitivity to coworkers and subordinates. They seek out their mentors. Women in business, unfortunately, will be experiencing the peculiar double standard a while longer—nothing changes overnight—but that doesn't mean that they must accept that standard. Those women just entering the workforce, or those who have been there and want to get more out of it, could do well to examine why some of their younger female counterparts have already made it. The traits these trendsetters possess don't necessarily have to be the exclusive preserve of young successes.

———

Lurking behind the abundance of pitfalls, insecurities, problems, obstacles and misconceptions inherent in young success is a very basic question: is it worth it? Does early achievement necessarily bring happiness? Are today's young achievers any happier than average or non-achievers? In daydreams, people often think that if only they had a new car or bigger house or larger office or fatter bankbook or more respect their problems would be solved—or at least greatly lessened. We look at someone who has youth, energy, some money, many plans and good position and think that person must be happy. Not to be happy in that situation would be positively un-American.

After the daydreams cease, most of us come to the sensible and inevitable conclusion that success—just like wealth or material things—does not in and of itself bring the elusive happiness we all strive for. Objects or position or financial security do not remove worry, doubt or ignorance and create security, confidence and knowledge in their stead. As we have seen, the attainment of success, with its added responsibilities and considerations, only brings further complications to an individual.

To expect achievement to make us happy is to miss the whole point of achieving. The young successes perhaps do have an edge on happiness in one important area: they know that in order to achieve exterior success and feel inner satisfaction, they must first harness and channel the internal resources— good and bad—that all of us possess. Their body of self-knowledge and courage to risk change has been a lifelong process, evolving slowly (for them) and painfully at times. They know that happiness comes to those who can solve their problems from within and not to those who expect some exterior trapping or achievement to do the job for them.

To many of us, happiness implies love. Do the young successes have the edge here? Not necessarily. Some of them, of course, had solid and happy family lives with husbands or wives and children or at least one enduring relationship. But there were a few with wives or husbands and children who were not as happy as the others. One young businessman worried that his hard-working life-style tended to preclude any romantic involvement. He spoke wistfully of wanting to have someone with whom to establish a lasting relationship. But another equally young and hard-driving businessman was more pragmatic: love could wait and, if it came, would have to work itself around his business. Some were selfish, others giving and loving. In this area young successes were no different from the rest of us.

Most of the achievers, however, did describe themselves as basically happy. At the same time, they realized that their restless nature and one-more-goal-before-sunset approach would mean that they might never be entirely satisfied. This they were perfectly willing to accept, following Robert Browning's view that "a man's reach should exceed his grasp,/Or what's a heaven for?"

If there was one area where an achiever had the inside track on happiness, it was in expectations of success. They didn't expect to get out of success any more than what they put into it: much hard work, love of challenge, an enthusiasm for the job to be done, a delight in achieving for its own sake. They seemed infinitely happier in their work, with its responsibilities, confrontations and brick walls, than most other people. This was probably because their restless nature wouldn't let them stay in an unhappy situation for very long.

The young successes were able to enjoy themselves and their lives because they enjoyed their work, because they had worked hard to get what they had and because they had done it on their own initiative. Very, very few of the achievers were wealthy enough to be able to "retire" and frolic; the realization that they would probably be working the rest of their lives— and that they truly *enjoyed* working and wanted to work—had been inbred very early. The young successes had no desire to beachcomb. They were happy, not because they had money or certain power or property, but because they were using their talents, brains, emotions and capabilities to their fullest. If there is one special kind of happiness in young success, it is that.

# 6 ≣ Innovation and Image

IT'S CERTAIN THAT factors such as social change, the economy and population shifts have all combined to create a climate where early achievement is more likely than in the past. But have those few who have already made it to the top young—in their own business or someone else's—made any difference? Do they conduct themselves and their organizations any differently from those older people who have traditionally held their positions? Are these young people erasing the ills of working in America, ills against which their generation so vociferously protested? Early successes represent the best their generation has to offer. And they hold the answer as to whether their generation of workers is full of bite—or bombast.

Ray Hickok, who founded the Young Presidents Organization in 1951, is fond of saying that cosmetic change must often take place before a lasting one. In many respects that is the position in which many fire-eating young of the Sixties now find themselves. Many seem to have adapted to the way things have always been done: the story of the Sixties radical leader who is now selling insurance in Colorado, or participating in a management trainee program at IBM or Bank of America, is almost a cliché. Former bomb throwers and demonstrators who hardly had time for a beansprout sandwich are now dropping $50 for business lunches.

But these people haven't sold out completely, and the way things have always been done is gradually beginning to change because of them. The most important aspect of influence of the young is the end of a certain kind of group-think. Traditional group-think, with its concern only for achieving a good bottom line, has yielded to group-think about the most socially conscious way to achieve a good bottom line—still group-think, granted, and probably open to abuse, but a change, all the same. Of course, the attitudes in older, established conglomerates are less likely to yield to immediate change than those in younger, smaller companies, but the concept of accountability and some degree of social responsibility is taking hold.

At the same time, the attitude of young people in power has changed. Their thoughts about that power, society, life-style and themselves, as well as the follies and strengths of youth, have been tempered by turbulent times and economic challenge. If their generation was idealistic, even naive about what it could accomplish, it was nevertheless one of the more realistic generations of young we have produced because of its battles—both won and lost. The result has been a deeper questioning of the way things are done and a courage to question and change them if those things come up short. Young people in power share one strong trait: they question conventional wisdom with unprecedented sharpness and cockiness. The young of previous generations have questioned, too, but this generation is in the position to do more than just inquire. It can instigate. And change.

Such change becomes apparent in small ways, something as simple and innovative as Steven Lefler displaying glass mugs in his stores in barrels on the floor instead of the conventional shelves. Or it can show up in significant structural changes within an institution: William George of Litton Industries questioned the twenty-four- to 40-month time period usually required to introduce a new product in the appliance industry. He cut that time by nine to eighteen months and got a jump on his market.

Perhaps change evolves because it is just easier for the young to get away with this sort of thing. Leon Botstein admits he can "drop a lot of the convention that comes with the job" as president of Bard College because of his age. Even so, innovative ability backed up the suggestions of his youth: in three years, he has already changed radically many procedures at the institution. First, he invented an unusual admission process called Immediate Decision, wherein a prospective Bard student studies a sixty-page syllabus of classical material incorporating philosophy, history, arts and science. The student then comes to campus and participates in a three-hour seminar on ethics and obedience to authority, using the syllabus material. While the student is participating, a faculty committee is studying his or her transcript, essays and letters of recommendation. At the end of the day, the student not only has had an input in the intellectual process, but also finds out if he or she has been accepted for admission.

Aware of the mistrust and misconceptions that lie on both ends of the generation gap, the young Botstein has sought to integrate students, faculty and members of the community. He formed a Center for Intergenerational Learning at Bard, non-credit courses in which old and young, students, faculty and local residents participate by discussing social and educational issues. At the same time, Botstein might seem to go back to older educational principles in his efforts to reform Bard's liberal arts curriculum to include serious study of the sciences and active arts. He was able in doing all these projects to incorporate both "old" and "young" ideas, and make them work.

Often people have fewer expectations of someone who is young and in a position of power. This, by extension, often allows that person to get away with a lot more than an older colleague might. And sometimes it works splendidly. Eugene D. Jackson had to use all his skill and incorporate the unflagging optimism that youth provides when he sought to form a radio network four years ago. He had a lot going against him, too: no new radio network had been formed in the United States since ABC started one in 1942; millions of dollars would need to be raised. But Jackson, a Kansas City man with degrees from the University of Missouri at Rolla and an MBA from Columbia University, knew he could succeed. He had been serving in the area of minority economic development for five years, specializing in minority venture capital. He raised the money while more faint hearts stood by with looks of disbelief, and formed the National Black Network, providing news shows, commentaries and other programs to radio stations with predominantly black audiences. It was a good investment and a good field for a young man. Today NBN grosses about $3 million each year, making the 33-year-old Jackson the most powerful black executive in the communications industry.

Like Botstein and Jackson, California businessman Norman Spaulding also used his youthful energy to good advantage in changing the status quo. When Spaulding took over his Eastmont mall project, he was not intimidated by how things had been done. He developed a computerized accounting system to replace a ten-year-old inefficient one the business had been using; he fired 68 of 75 employees; he replaced the mall's faulty security agency. To involve the community in his business, he instituted an Oakland school project in retailing based at the center, and scheduled free gospel concerts and church-sponsored charity bazaars. Within two years, Spaulding's innovation had created the first profit in the center's ten-year history.

Such success stems from the need of today's young working generation to be slightly different and to question more. That generation has another important need: to be more career- than work-oriented. The sense of "me" is firmly implanted. Work becomes something more than just hours one must put in in order to collect enough money to live. Instead, work must be in some way meaningful, satisfying. The prototype young success emerging from the jumble of the Sixties has a strong need to identify with the product, service or institution for which he or she works.

James L. Hayes, President of the American Management Association, has seen this increasing personal emphasis in the recent crop of MBAs and thinks it a good thing. He says that the young managers of the seventies:

> Are more aware than managers of previous generations of the carryover between business life and personal life. In many cases, they are no longer a part of the city in which the office is located. They are very much a part of a suburban life. Recognition at home arises out of their abilities as a person and less out of the significance of where they work. Young people do not want to go home after work and kick the cat because they left some part of their self-esteem or dignity on the job—perhaps as food for someone's hungry ego.
>
> They realize if they allow themselves to be diminished on the job, they will find their personal lives diminished, too. This is a fallout of the problem solving technique—the dignity and sense of accomplishment that comes from solving problems through good logic and not necessarily with the aid of total recall or memorizing. Our younger managers are interested in a total lifestyle that preserves their dignity, builds their self-esteem and accords them a feeling of freedom.

As one symptom of this change, it seems that second-year law students from Ivy League universities are no longer rushing to the portals of large Wall Street firms for the prestige and security they offer. Instead such prominent firms are often finding themselves going out as much as a year ahead to recruit the graduates they want. John Jay Osborn, a Harvard Law graduate and author of *The Paper Chase*, recalls one Columbia law student who divided his summer between an established Wall Street firm and a smaller one in Houston—the latter at half his New York salary. The student was willing to sacrifice the money he could be making in the East for the more open atmosphere and flexible life-style of the West. The fact that more and more law clerks are asking for less impersonal work environments and more people-oriented life-styles has not been lost upon the larger, established law firms. One such firm, in a letter to students at Yale, stresses the fact that "we have a personality and a way of doing things all our own. Our style and approach tends to be informal." The "me" generation strikes again!

As one result, when this Sixties-influenced generation does get in the position of running a business, it tends to administrate in a more participatory, more people-oriented way. Adman Ted Chin speaks of "creating an environment where people could feel important and make the contributions they were capable of, an environment that brings out the very best in other human beings." Discussing his days as *Esquire* editor, Lee Eisenberg talks about the "greater humanity in the way I ran the office. I think there was an openness there. It was a willingness on my part to show an emotional side." At Litton Industries, William George put theory into practice by introducing "sensing sessions," dialogues with his 600 hourly employees to make them feel more a part of the decision-making process.

Myron Taylor, in his midthirties a vice president of the Morgan Guaranty Trust Company in New York, is typical of young successes of the new generation. When asked about his ambitions, he speaks in terms of the hopes he has for those who work for him:

> I think from a managerial perspective. I want to mold a department where creativity and character are traits that permeate the environment—where individuals develop a sense of camaraderie—and where the collective, creative will of its members mesh into a single entity. That's what I want to bring to the managerial structure.

Like many young chargers, David A. Bloomfield recognizes that restlessness is not always such a bad thing. As vice president and general manager of the Ruco division of Hooker Chemicals and Plastics Corporation, he was profiled by *Business Week* as one example of the new, young top management in industry. "I tend to get people with strong ambitions who may be likely to leave after a couple of years, but if they do I know they will leave a strong organization behind," he says. That is partially due to the fact that he divided his $80-million operation into segments and gives each manager profit responsibility and the autonomy necessary to deal with the problems. Again, an emphasis on people.

Such an emphasis is coupled with a heightened consciousness of what the image of business has been, and what the image of business could be if tempered by the zeal of the Sixties. Joe Armstrong, who left his post at *Rolling Stone* to assume the presidency of the New York Magazine Corporation, has a management style and ensuing consciousness typical of those in his successful generation. And it is a style that takes some heretofore unconventional elements into account. Armstrong has faith in his instincts, and says he hires people on the basis of chemistry, instinct and energy, for such qualities are just as, if not more, important as knowledge or past experience. He is acutely aware of the style of publishing moguls in the past, and speaks of his desire not to repeat their mistakes: "You hear about everybody who's been a legend in publishing or made a significant impact," he says, "a Hearst or a Luce or somebody like that. They've all had a real bastard side, a cruel side, a selfish side. I want to prove that you can do it and be successful and you can treat other people like you want to be treated and you don't have to be cruel and selfish to achieve the same end result."

Are such observations mere lip service, or do such young successes really run their businesses that way? And are their peers taking a cue from them for the future? One successful young lawyer says they are—but with certain reservations:

> Basically, we're doing things a little bit differently, which is why it's succeeding. That's why the radical movement in the Sixties had failed and never has been heard of since, and why a certain element of the Sixties has survived—because it does things not that dramatically different from their elders but enough different. There are some things that will last: the feeling of equality of men and women will last. The feeling of not wanting too much will last. I don't see my peers who are very successful as money-grubbing. Now, they are money-grubbing, but not as money-grubbing as in the past. They're embarrassed to talk about the accumulation of capital for its own sake. It's not to say that they don't do it. It's not to say that my friends who make it don't buy yachts—they do. But they at least justify it differently and probably are more reluctant to do it. I think successful people today generally have more of a soul than comparable successes of ten or fifteen years ago. I think we're making a difference, but it's less of a difference than some people think. It's a quantum leap, but it's not utopian.

Ah, but vive la différence. It shows up first in what the baby-boom generation lists as desirable in a job. Since the bulk of today's younger adults have lived in a time where material well being was not too much of a concern, at least not like it was during the Depression or war years, they are demanding more from business. They are demanding early, if not immediate, responsibility in a job. They are looking for risk and challenge for their talents. They want a meaningful voice in making decisions where they work. Their need to be treated as an individual, not as a number or a member of a stereotyped group, is important. And when achievement is attained, they want to be recognized for it. Their work must be meaningful, and provide some outlet for self-expression.

These things are what people are asking for, but do they get them? Since the modus operandi of corporations doesn't move as quickly as the dreams and ambition of youth, chances are the young man or woman looking to find all the elements in one job will be somewhat disappointed in the main. But the big difference is that more people are willing to go elsewhere to find more of these elements. Gone are the days of being indentured to a company until death does one part. Even as traditional a company as Procter & Gamble says in its recruiting literature that the first employer is no longer looked upon as a person's career employer. Such a change in attitude—both on the part of impatient idealistic employee and realistic employer —has created a new phenomenon in the business world: job hopping. Once the exclusive preserve of fast-moving sectors like advertising agencies or television networks, hopping from job to job has invaded all sectors of business life. Bright young men and women these days often make four or five job moves before their 30th birthday. Years ago, personnel directors would look askance at a résumé that had four job changes in so short a time. But that has changed.

Those who hop, hop for many reasons. Many jump ship for salary changes. Some companies are reporting the rehiring of employees who left years ago to drive their marketability up, rehiring them at a salary much higher than they would have been making had they stayed with the company originally. Others change for more responsibility, or more job satisfaction. Whatever the reason, at its base is the need to be personally satisfied and the realization, borne partly of Sixties turbulence, that one does not have to forever languish as in the past. Job-hopping is becoming a given, and it is the symptom of a generation's need to identify. Management consultant G. William Moore simply grins that "the Sixties generation isn't going to deal with 'Massa' anymore. They're not indentured." And Moore has statistics to prove it: 75 percent of all management development trainees a large corporation will hire today, he says, will not be in that corporation five years from now.

Such leaping from job to job is not the exclusive preserve of those just starting out in business. Jumping ship is becoming more common at the highest corporate levels. In the past, chief executive officers were married to their companies until they were ousted. It was not common for a CEO to go to another company in a comparable position. Instead, the CEO was "bought off" or shuffled to a less important position on the side. But the shortage of "properly aged" CEO candidates has changed that. The result is a form of executive musical chairs. Lester B. Korn's Korn/Ferry International, an executive recruiting firm, has reported that its demand for supplying top corporate officers has increased steadily in recent years.

Young achievers go right along with the job-hop pattern. A full 25 percent of those interviewed had changed jobs between their interviews and publication. Most had switched to more lucrative jobs within their professions; some had switched professions entirely. All who switched—and even those who hadn't —indicated that job changes were inevitable for them. With their love of challenge, openness to new opportunities and in-bred restlessness, staying in the same position, albeit successful position, was somehow unthinkable.

Switching jobs with frequency can have its dark side, of course. Some corporations might be reluctant to spring for elaborate training programs without the assurance that those they train will be there to return benefits to the company. Too many job changes can have a negative effect for a young restless employee and make finding a new job that much harder. There is certainly the danger that some eager young employees will be too eager, leaving a job too soon before they have fully learned it. Perhaps he or she is searching for an employment utopia that doesn't exist, or perhaps has difficulties adjusting to situations on the job. Some observers, like YPO's Ray Hickok, think that too frequent job changes are symptomatic of deeper problems. Hickok laments that "so many young people are not willing to blame themselves. They're willing to blame the Establishment, everything around them, and not lay the burden of responsibility on their own shoulders." There are those who think that often the need for self-fulfillment can lead to self-indulgence. Frequent job hops may help some young whizzes learn the system faster, but are they learning it well enough? Is job-hopping a symptom of a basic laziness, a lack of stick-to-it-ness?

If it is or isn't depends on the individual, but there is agreement that proper job-hopping can be an instructive and positive force for employee and employer. Still, corporations don't relish the loss of bright young talent. So to make sure budding geniuses stay within the corporate fold, many businesses have altered traditional ways of dealing with their employees. Hiring an older manager in a "caretaker" position is one way to show young employees there will be a place for them when they are ready. Often, when a younger person is the head of the corporation, he or she will go to extraordinary lengths to prove to the young up-and-comers that there is still a chance. Samuel Casey, Jr., President and Chief Executive Officer of Pullman, Inc., did just that. In 1970 when he was 43, he wrote out his own resignation, signed it and dated it ten years in the future. He did it, he said, to show his younger executives that they should not stop their own rush for the top.

The American Management Association's Hayes, however,

believes that a young/old combination in business is a fertile one, if certain procedures are followed for mutual consideration:

> It would only be fair to observe that many of the young managers and many of the "old" managers in both government and business have teamed up very constructively—the old manager learning a bit about the new sciences and the young manager quickly gathering the fruit of experience. A little more "honesty" on both sides, however, would remove much of the unnecessary tensions that currently exist between generations. For example, the superior may claim that he manages by objective and doesn't worry about how you get there. But when there is a mystique in an unusual solution, the superior definitely cares how the young person got there. Older managers can feel insecure if too much "newness" appears without advance notice. The new manager can do much to eliminate these suspicions and feelings of insecurity by simply informing a superior of a new procedure beforehand, and the rationale for it.

Things are changing. Age per se is not as large a factor in business as it once was, and its importance has assumed a new shape and definition. In spite of the generation gap, the older executive has become more willing to accept a young person in a responsible position. This is due in part to the fact that the same shortage of older executives which makes hiring and promoting young chargers a necessity has at the same time created a renaissance for the older generation as well. Experience is valued, and in demand. Industry, law, academic institutions, finance, publishing—all can now hire a young lion or lioness for positions where risk-taking, energy and vision are needed. At the same time they can bring aboard an older person for those jobs requiring more experience, judgment and a long-term view. Ironically, often the hiring of an older manager or executive helps the company to keep its younger employees.

This strategy in effect tells the young employee that there is still hope for advancement. It is not uncommon for large corporations to attract senior outsiders to keep the organization running smoothly, while letting those young executives "in waiting" mature a few years more.

It is also not uncommon to see corporations headed by younger people lead the way in hiring the "elders." The young successes interviewed spoke with pride about hiring a 60-year-old vice president or a 55-year-old associate. These employers were eager to show that they knew in what areas age and experience were valuable and in what areas risktaking could apply. In the hiring of these older employees and managers, they were making a sound business decision without regard for societal stereotypes. The young didn't just hire the young, nor was responsibility and upward mobility the exclusive preserve of these peoples' contemporaries. They tended to base their hiring on the individual, not the age group.

Business people—young and old—are realizing that the compacted experience and better educational skills of the young makes it unnecessary to force the young to stay in one position as long as they had in the past. Executives, professors, lawyers, administrators and bankers are not waiting as long for advancement as they did a few years ago. Their employers are realizing that people can learn a position and advance faster than ever before. Traditional corporate barriers to promotion have been broken down and the young are moving more rapidly through the hierarchy. The older executives brought in today play an important role of caretaker for the company. They know that the young will take it over soon enough. Such concessions to the young, and consideration of the old, is a direct result of a shifting population base coupled with the changing consciousness of business. Ability, not age, is creating new avenues of promotion and hiring.

This state of affairs should affect not just the corporate

boardroom and executive suite. In a utopian setup it would mean that in the future there would be no "old" or "young" jobs, that people would be hired and placed according to their abilities, not age. Carried to the extreme, it could remove the uncomfortable feeling we have when working with someone who is either an exceptional achiever or a below-average achiever. People could work at their own pace and not feel unhappy about how old they are vis-à-vis their jobs. The average achiever wouldn't labor under the fear that if he or she didn't learn the job in three years that that would be held against the record and block further advancement. On the other hand, the above-average-achiever would know that if he or she learned the job in six months instead of three years, early promotion wouldn't be out of the question.

That situation has not been reached yet, of course, and the resignation letter of Samuel Casey, while it might be an extreme, points toward what has become a new and disturbing trend for companies—young, talented workers leaving established business altogether.

Those who elect to stay within the corporate structure stay to change it incrementally. Such young achievers strive to make their bailiwicks more responsive to their employees and more responsible socially. But there are only so many positions open for innovators, young or old, in the corporate structure. American industry has stopped the rapid growth of the go-go Sixties and pulled back. What happens to the job-hopper who finds even a slightly changed corporate structure unacceptable? What does an achiever do when he or she cannot move as quickly as his or her talents and ambition dictate?

Often they drop out of the structure altogether, going into business for themselves. Circumstances of population, economics and a changing business climate that is not changing fast enough for some young chargers of the "me" generation are of necessity creating a new generation of entrepreneurs. If the need to identify with one's work, to be more people oriented and more concerned with socially responsive issues is not filled to one's satisfaction, the likely answer is to go into business for oneself and show the world how it's done. The Bureau of Labor Statistics, which keeps track of such things, notes a definite upswing in people starting their own businesses in the early and mid-1970s. The prognosis for small businesses in this country is never as good as the entrepreneur might wish—at last glance it was estimated that a depressing 50 percent of all small businesses started in America fail. But never before have the economic and social climates combined to produce a new and somewhat forced generation of go-it-alone business pioneers.

Such a need to strike out on one's own has affected even the most established institutions of higher learning. Early in 1977 three of the nation's top business schools—Harvard, Wharton School of Finance and Stanford University—announced they were going out of their way to recruit potential entrepreneurs and those interested in smaller businesses. Long the prime source of future executives for large American corporations, such schools have realized that there are many students who are not soured on the concepts of business but wish business to be more scaled to their needs. In February, 1977, recognizing that many of their students might not want to be lost in the vast corporate caverns of an IBM or General Foods, Harvard Business School for the first time in its history held a recruiting day for businesses that were managed by six or fewer executives. The Sixties influence on a generation is showing that small can not only be beautiful, but it can be satisfying and profitable as well.

The creation of an enlightened entrepreneurship is not just a concept. There exists a loosely knit network of new entrepreneurs in America, people who adhere to E. F. Schumacher's premise that to make "a right livelihood," work should not just provide financial assistance but also room for development of self and the environment. Such counterculture capitalists, be they accountants or herbal-tea wholesalers, are laying the groundwork for a business climate in which business is not a bad word. Such a band of rugged individualists and their peculiar pragmatic idealism even has its own business seminar. In June, 1977, the Tarrytown House Executive Conference Center created a three-week course entitled "School for Entrepreneurs." The course cost $400 and was immediately filled by men and women in their 20s and 30s. In an atmosphere one writer described as "resembling a mixture of a Buddhist monastery and the Harvard Business School," the two dozen budding entrepreneurs struggled with concepts of risk-taking, marketing strategies and profit margins. They made it known that they would not become stereotypical young executives selling their skills to the highest bidder, that their businesses would reflect their own values.

Whether or not that will happen remains to be seen, but such young pioneers have taken a large step toward creating their own business ethic. Perhaps they will give birth to the "confederation of entrepreneurs" that Norman Macrae, deputy editor of the Economist, sees as inevitable. Macrae predicts that the era of large corporations is fizzling out, and that their giant bureaucracies will be replaced by entrepreneurial confederations that would be marked by flexibility, intimacy and high production and efficiency. Macrae even gives a timetable for the concept, saying that between 1975 and 2010 corporations will radically change their form. The labor pains are already being felt.

As America enters an era when the four-day work week is more than an idea, where leisure time is more plentiful, there will be new markets created for small businesses. Such conditions could be auspicious for a generation raised in turmoil, realism and idealism as well. The new news, then, is that young entrepreneurs will be attacking big business by developing small business, a trend observers view with great excitement. The new generation of entrepreneurs was weaned on risk and competition and the importance of work being tailored to the individual. The American Success Dream has been slightly altered. The work ethic continues, but with a new twist.

＝

Just how much change is happening and how much will happen depends, of course, on the profession and the people within it. Young, dynamic successes seem to pop up in business, especially in those younger, trendier businesses that have more flexible structures. However, as we have seen, there are early achievers in powerful positions in more established "super" corporations. Business is not the only area that has felt the impact of the baby-boom successes: academia—in administration and tenure—has seen a new crop of younger power-holders. So have the law firms and law schools. So have financial institutions—Wall Street, the banks, investment firms. So has the publishing world—editors, agents, wheeler-dealers are younger. As all professions adjust to the tastes and realize the buying power of the influential baby boomers, more and more members of that generation will be taking faster routes to power. Such avenues are open, seemingly for the first time, to those who just a few short years ago would have been considered "too young" for the job.

In the same spirit, innovation does not have to be the exclusive preserve of youth. Their inherent sense of risk and youth paid off, of course. But one does not have to be young to take risks or try something new. The move toward a new work ethic, incorporating career instead of job orientation, participation by all workers, and more room for appreciation of individual effort has at the same time removed many of the stigmas of age—at the high and low end of the scale. A young executive who has felt age discrimination because he or she was thought "too young" will be more likely to be sympathetic to workers and executives who are now told they are "too old" for advancement.

It is easier today to escape from a stifling or unrewarding job than it was, say, twenty years ago. There are more choices now, and the stigma of leaving a job or career which traps one is fading. Job hopping is not just for those young people starting out. The quest for satisfaction and fulfillment in one's work has enabled many older workers to grow, to change—and, in many instances, to reenter the work force. The young, restless job-jumper merely cleared the way. Such young successes have shown that the creation of change can be a realistic goal, and that's an important cue to take for the future.

# 7 ▤ Making It Today

• The deck is stacked in favor of the tried and proven way of doing things and against the taking of risks and striking out in new directions.
—John D. Rockefeller III

• The mass of managers of a corporation no longer have a viable map into the future. The whole system is filled with a degree of uncertainty we did not have in the 1960s, when we still had the belief that the future is basically benevolent and management is solving today's problems and that tomorrow will take care of itself. Today we know the future is malevolent, which is another way to say that today there is an increasing number of ways in which you can screw up and only a few ways in which you can look intelligent. It's like Murphy's Law except we have a new law called O'Garrity's Law which says that Murphy was an optimist.
—Eugene Jennings

AT FIRST GLANCE, the concept of "making it" might seem to the Seventies what "peace and love" was to the Sixties and "don't rock the boat" was to the Fifties. There are books on power and how to get and keep it, books on being assertive, books on the care and feeding of success. Such emphasis on self-help, self-improvement and self-fulfillment has come about not only as a result of a cultural shift in attitudes toward work and one another, but also as a result of economic and social necessity. Competition is fierce. The economy is no longer in the rapid growth pattern of the Sixties. The job market is relatively static in spite of new leisure time activities opening up. The ranks of the baby-boom babies have swollen the workforce to unprecedented proportions, creating unprecedented unemployment as a consequence. Although there have been major changes in the way America conducts its business, and treats its employees, these changes have not happened quickly enough. Opportunity, while still there for the grabbing, remains the same when the numbers demand it expand. Such a situation has created a time bomb of frustration and anger for those in the "good times/bad times" generation of the Sixties.

One successful young publishing executive, not entirely tongue-in-cheek, speaks of the people in his generation who, disillusioned, leave their offices after their fantastic climbs: "I can see them leaving just as happily with a bomb behind them as walking out the door." That is not to say we have given birth to a generation of mad bombers. Indeed, many of the executive's radical friends are now slogging it out in the conventional world of commerce and familial responsibility. But we have created a shifting economic, social, cultural and business climate in which the rules change as quickly as the teams and individuals learn to play them. Although such questioning, upheaval, turmoil and change are good, a residue of confusion is left behind. The way out of such confusion, which has hit each generation with varying degree but seems to be accentuated in the wake of the Sixties, is never easy. As it has been in the past, the way out of the confusion of the Sixties/Seventies will be discovered by leaders, strong leaders who have perspective to see through the muck, energy to help clear it and vision to create something better. Those who have become successful young in America these days, those who have risen above the obstacles of competition and conditioning and made it all work for them, have such strong leadership qualities. In many ways they are not only clearing the path for the leaders of tomorrow, they are the leaders of tomorrow.

The problem is that still more leaders are needed, in a time when—ironically—education, society and business breed followers and team players. At a 1976 conference on leadership, Consumer Advocate Ralph Nader explained some of the reasons why this country seems to have produced so many team players and, in some conferees' opinion, a resulting lack of leaders with vision:

> The family and other private order institutions fulfilled a much greater function years ago than now. Our reliance for a good society has been thrown onto public and private corporations, unions, government (which) are expert at diffusing responsibility and accountability and are not being touched by the same moral standards as individuals are.

Nader is not alone in questioning the effects of a "progressive" and bureaucratic society. Psychologists, writers, business leaders and other observers of contemporary mores have worried aloud about the dissolution of the nuclear family and the assuming of the traditional family roles by outside institutions. Historian Christopher Lasch, in describing what he terms "The Narcissistic Personality of Our Time," speaks of a basic shift in socialization, previously the work of the family unit. Through the miracle of mass production and as a result of an industrial society, the socializing functions of the family have been taken over by the advertising industry, the schools, the mental health

and welfare services. Governmental agencies, in the guise of helping people lead better lives, may instead take away from them in-
advertently the responsibilities so important to the formation of
leadership. It becomes harder and harder for an individual to
take control of his or her own life. Lasch maintains these forces
and agencies have allied themselves with the younger generation
against the older, so that the desires of the young supersede
those of their parents. As a result, the family is organized around
the requirements of a self-indulgent future generation. This re-
moves in part another essential area for achievement: the recognition of the talents of those who are older and the desire to
learn from them as a consequence. Such an undermining of rural
values, the old-style family and individualism has created a situation in which the work ethic has been replaced by a "fun moral-
ity," which is essentially narcissistic—and not the best breed-
ing ground for future leaders with a strong set of values and
goals. Political apathy and intellectual apathy result; the potential for leadership and achievement is societally diminished.

A bureaucratic society arising from the desire to meet the
needs of the greatest number of people, then, may inadverently
undermine the strongest part of that society: the delicate area
that gives us aware, self-determined people who have the potential to become tomorrow's leaders. When so many forces
have a stake in the individual's life, the need to attain the
"hunger" that drives one to achieve, is deemphasized as an in-
advertent consequence of the societal good. Harvard Business
School Professor Abraham Zaleznik speaks of a "new power
ethic that favors collective over individual leadership, the cult
of the group over that of personality."

Traditionally, good economic times and a technological oriented society tend to depreciate the need for strong leaders.
In such times, reasoning has it, it is more important to create
an atmosphere conducive to maintaining the status quo smoothly
than to emphasize areas of society that might produce strong

risk-takers guaranteed to rock the boat. Traditionally, periods of stress—a Depression or World War—tend to point out the sharp differences between managers and leaders, and heighten the need for the latter.

Society functions with both, indeed, needs both if it is to survive. The times, however, dictate whether leaders of managers should be nurtured. Managers perpetuate the group. Their need for survival dominates their need for risk. They prefer working with people, with a set structure that it is their job to maintain. They are devoted to making sure the process moves smoothly and efficiently. In order to effectively solve problems, they act to limit the number of choices available, to make those choices manageable. Leaders, on the other hand, are by nature involved. They represent ideas and identify personally with the goal rather than with the process. They work from high-risk positions, developing fresh approaches and working to expand options instead of limit them. Leaders and managers can complement each other, and need each other as much as the system needs both of them.

But the laws of supply and demand apply equally to leaders and managers as they do to guns and butter. And like it or not we have become a nation of managers in a time that cries out for leaders in a way not seen before. The Seventies scenario is one of decent economic times set in a highly technological society. Yet for all the prosperity, the Seventies dangerously resemble the Depression years, when jobs were scarce and applicants plentiful. In the midst of the Seventies, people look for an explanation of such an uneasy coexistence. *Time* magazine holds a conference on leadership asking prominent writers, politicians and educators a practically unanswerable question: how do you create leaders in a country that is geared to creating managers? Joe McGinniss, one of the youngest authors to ever make the best-seller list (for his trailbreaking *Selling of the President 1968*) in 1975 goes on a search for heroes in America. He concludes that they are all gone and sadly quotes Norman Mailer: "There is only a modern hero, damned by no more than the ugliness of wishes whose satisfaction he will never know."

Perhaps there are no more heroes in the traditional mode. But Mailer's modern hero could be tomorrow's leader; with he or she (for now the definition of heroes and leaders cannot be exclusively limited to men) searching for an elusive goal, yet searching for it with energy and vision nonetheless, a nation of managers is given a new path to follow. And those who best fit Mailer's definition, whose wishes, ugly or not, are never satisfied, are the young achievers. They are our best and, some might argue, last stronghold of self-determinism, of the conventional work ethic. They possess, for all their faults, the spirit of independence and achievement that we need in our leaders.

If achievers seem to be in short supply, as they traditionally are, can we create more leaders, instill in them the qualities of those who have become successful early? Are we capable of creating overachievers to meet society's needs for vision and leadership? Unfortunately, the answer is no. It is impossible to manufacture leaders as one manufactures toothpaste. It is impossible to educate someone for leadership as we educate someone to be a doctor or lawyer. Leaders, overachievers, early bloomers, young successes—whatever the term used to describe them—are formed in spite of the system, not because of it. In many cases, as we have seen, it is necessary to have the abrasion of a society geared to the status quo to create the pearl of uniqueness, of individuality. That dichotomy of ostensibly educating for independence while encouraging conformity is painfully necessary. No, it will never be possible to send a bright young man or woman to "achiever school" in order to turn out leaders for the future. There are simply too many individual quirks to consider, too many possible avenues to explore, leading to self-confidence and achievement. To distill all of that neatly into a curriculum is a Herculean—and foolish—undertaking.

If society can't consciously train a leader, then how will this country fill its need for young ambitious successes who have the daring and ideals to cope with and solve the difficult problems facing America in the future? We may not be able to stamp out leaders like Christmas cookies, but we can do some things to make sure that a potential overachiever, a potential leader, is encouraged and nourished. It is first important to create an atmosphere in which being different—an already "difficult" situation for which there is no "remedy"—is not punished. That is not as easy as it seems. Our society says it values the individual and his or her uniqueness. But that value drops when the individual is truly different: a young schoolgirl who speaks two or three languages is ostracized by her classmates for being "strange"; a young boy who excels in class is sneered at, called a "brain" by his peers. Schools are predicated on the idea of teaching how things are done, which is fine. But the other function of academic life, that of inquiry, of adding to present knowledge, is often not as encouraged as much as it could be. "Radical" ideas are frowned upon and laughed at, as teachers forget that many of today's accepted theories were once themselves poohpoohed.

When those who are "different" leave school with their body of knowledge, they enter a workplace for the most part devoted to perpetuating the status quo. A whole new body of regulations emerges, in which the chances for taking responsibility for one's work are limited. Hours are stiffly regulated, although flexible hours are now being tried by some companies who realize their employees can be useful and productive in something other than a nine-to-five time slot. There are myriad rules of dress and conduct. Peer pressure—to look "hip" or to look like a somber banker—is as intense as pressure in school to dress like everybody else and blend in with the "right" crowd. The work itself frequently leaves little room for experimentation and imagination. "That's the way it is. That's the way it has always been done" are phrases an employee recites in his sleep. The constraints to productivity and innovation are a constant: society has not only decreed that one is not capable of reason, imagination and responsibility at a young age, but that the same individual will not be capable of same in old age. Sixty-five is the cutoff point for "official" usefulness, though this will be generously expanded to 70 or older as the population base gets older, reflecting an aging baby-boom generation.

Of course, education is necessary. So are rules of behavior and procedure governing the conduct of people at home and in the workplace. But when these rules infringe upon an individual's right to grow and prosper, when they interfere with an individual's achieving his or her intellectual and social potential, then it is time for society to take a second look at its constraints on individual growth, as it looks at barriers to its own economic growth.

It is time to question whether such rules are there to perpetuate the common good or simply the safe status quo. An historical perspective must be reached. Civilizations prosper with new ideas, and wither with endless repetition of old ones. Times change. The Sixties in many ways jolted America. Often that jolt was followed by contempt for those who advocated radical change. As change emerging from the Sixties will be of necessity incremental, so will the change in attitude toward those who are brighter, quicker, more imaginative and innovative than society is comfortable with at the time. But such tolerance must come if we are to create an atmosphere more conducive to the development of leaders. As a society, we must realize that a ten-year-old's ability to do advanced calculus or write a lucid novel does not diminish our ability to balance our checkbooks or write letters to loved ones. Unusual propensity toward achievement and accomplishment is not something to be feared or shunned, but something to be encouraged. For it eventually enriches those who most fear it.

If the function of an educational system is to provide the individual with a set body of knowledge with which to tackle the world, and if that world of necessity is fairly rigid in its structures, what can be done to encourage uniqueness in a practical way? Ironically, the most obvious and feasible starting point is the workplace, that bastion of institutionalization and the status quo. If companies are to survive, it is important that they keep their employees who have high potential, instead of losing such achievers to the ranks of the new entrepreneurs. What will eventually happen if high-potential employees are not encouraged and leave as a result? Pennsylvania State University business administration professor Robert A. Pitts paints a bleak picture:

> As the cream from the pool of younger talent is siphoned off by the loss of outstanding persons, a company must draw increasingly on personnel of mediocre and even inferior ability to staff higher level positions. As it does so, it gradually but inevitably commits itself to mediocrity.

To prevent such a mediocrity boom, it will be necessary for companies to initially identify who is a potential achiever and who is not. This is a tricky course, of necessity subjective. The formulation of standardized employee assessment guidelines is one way to separate the above average from the norm. One Fortune 500 company has created such a yardstick, a three-part reporting format that rates its managers on performance, potential and readiness for promotion. To help eliminate subjective judgments that vary from department to department, this company has made its assessment criteria company-wide policy. There will always be sources of bias, whatever the system. Some supervisors will be harsh, others lenient. Bad personal chemistry can influence assessment. Departmental prejudice—evaluating a candidate's performance only in terms of one department's functions—can also cloud the picture. Yet this company's system is serving as a valuable tool to identify future leaders. A sample assessment report of this particular company requires supervisors to judge an employee by the following criteria:

### PERFORMANCE

| | |
|---|---|
| 1—Outstanding | Exceptional achievement of goals and expectations. Excellent overall performance. |
| 2—Superior | Major goals and expectations achieved effectively. Consistent high performer. |
| 3—Competent | Achieved essential goals and expectations. Successful performance. |
| 4—Below Expectations | Achievement of goals and expectations is below acceptable level. Requires major investment. |
| 5—Unacceptable | Has not achieved goals and expectations. Has not responded to corrective efforts. |

### POTENTIAL

| | |
|---|---|
| 1—Blue | A potential division general manager. |
| 2—Green | Can do next job. |
| 3—Brown | Stay in specialty. |
| 4—Yellow | OK in current position, but no upward potential. |
| 5—Red | Marginal performer. |

### READINESS

| | |
|---|---|
| 1—Up—now | Ready for immediate promotion. |
| 2—Up-6 | Ready for promotion in 6 months. |
| 3—Up-12 | Ready for promotion in 12 months. |
| 4—Stay | Should remain in present position for more than 12 months (a) for more development or (b) because division needs him or her. |
| 5—Marginal | Marginal performer who should be terminated. |

Once above-average employees have been identified, what can and should be done with them? Often such employees will be boxed in to their departments. If they are young achievers, they will already be impatient for more responsibility and new challenges, having learned their jobs quickly. And they will probably be eager to jump ship. To keep them from doing just that, Robert Pitts proposes cross-divisional transfers for these identified hotshots. The employee will be transferred to a new division within the company where new responsibilities await. The achiever will be challenged by a new department and a new set of problems to solve. This approach can help everyone: the achiever is kept constructively occupied until other high responsibility positions ripe for his or her talents open up elsewhere in the company, and the company keeps a competent employee within the fold, out of the reach of competitors and the growing ranks of entrepreneurs challenging its territory.

Even simpler methods exist to encourage and nourish an achiever. Abraham Zaleznik speaks of the "myth" that people learn best from their peers. He questions strong peer orientation in companies, which he says tends to produce more managers than leaders. Why? Because an emphasis on one's contemporaries eliminates one factor often crucial to overachievers—a strong one-to-one relationship with an older executive who can challenge and teach the young up-and-comer. In short, the current highly sophisticated and staffed corporate structures make it very difficult for a young charger to have a mentor. Relaxing such established concepts as peer group task forces, resulting in a challenging interchange of older and younger executives, would do wonders to encourage the potential of the younger executive.

One admittedly high-risk position that some companies may be able to afford in order to prevent a talent drain is allowing the young charger to go up the ladder as he or she wishes, a position made more corporately acceptable as a result of the influence of the baby boom. Another is the simple tolerance of young—and threatening—subordinates by older executives. Zaleznik writes that intolerance of higher achievement types not only favors the creation of managers and stifles potential leaders, but can ultimately damage the company itself:

> To confront is also to tolerate aggressive interchange, and has the net effect of stripping away the veils of ambiguity and signalling so characteristic of managerial cultures, as well as encouraging the emotional relationship leaders need if they are to survive.

Companies must change not only to encourage leaders, but also to preserve its management. With an overabundance of young talent, fattened by the addition of women and minorities to the executive workforce, job security could loom as a volatile issue. If consumerism and corporate accountability were the large business issues of the Sixties and early Seventies, job security may well be the largest internal business issue of the late Seventies and early Eighties. Arch Patton, a former chairman of the Presidential Commission on Executive, Legislative, and Judicial Salaries, sees rising management self-interest in the next decade, as promotions are filled by younger people and are therefore held longer. Patton and others say that top corporate management must upgrade middle-level jobs before pressure by their employees to organize unions reaches a critical level. Companies must offer better pay (starting salaries are already softening for entry-level jobs because of the overabundance of qualified applicants), must streamline their decision-making processes and reduce their bureaucracies in order to effect faster and better decisions to match the force of the times and the level of their managerial talent. Not to institute such changes would have the effect of quashing management's basic right to manage. To not rethink policy could lead to the formation of strong management self-interest groups. If teachers, football players and doctors can form unions, so can middle management.

All such steps, to nourish achievers as well as protect the structure of business as we know it, imply risk. But in the face of the difficult problems of the next decade, leaders will be needed and change will be essential for survival. Young and old must take on the responsibility, for today's eager young chargers are tomorrow's more conservative citizens. Zaleznik writes that "the risks associated with power in the hands of an individual may be necessary ones for business to take if organizations are to break free of their inertia and bureaucratic conservatism"— and he is right. Such bureaucratic conservatism is not the exclusive preserve of business. Nor is the need to rethink policy and look for potential leaders. Academic institutions, with an over-abundance of professional talent facing a future of fewer upcoming students to receive it, can become as stratified and frustrating as corporations. Law schools turn out more lawyers than the system can absorb. Journalism schools turn out more writers and reporters than there are jobs to be filled. All institutions, responding to the vast educational and social needs of the baby-boom generation, contributed to the frustration of that generation. And all institutions—academic, business, social—must take heed of the generational time bomb in their midst and rethink their avenues to growth and prosperity. Achievers must be identified early, and encouraged early, if such institutions are to survive and grow and successfully face the increasing problems ahead.

An urgency for this is underlined in a passage from a Procter & Gamble recruiting booklet being given to today's young graduates. The booklet discusses steadily increasing pressures for sweeping change in U.S. business and industry, and acknowledges that in an era of rapid, far-reaching change it is possible for a company to "get hit on the blind side," being set back by an unanticipated force for change that could perpetuate a crisis. Its point:

> It is only with an organization filled with people who see change as desirable and necessary—a way of life—that constructive change can be brought about in an orderly and gradual fashion through self-initiative. And it is only with an organiza-

tion of people already change-oriented—people who even welcome the challenges of an *unanticipated* demand for change—that we can maintain our corporate equilibrium and come back strongly if knocked off balance by a 'blind side' blow.

Those "change oriented" people will come from the ranks of the high potential young achievers—if they can be identified in time.

And the task of identifying such comers will fall more and more to the personnel department. Long a forgotten department rated "soft" on the executive scale, personnel has been historically—and ironically—a favorite dumping ground for a company's women and minority employees. But the focus of the personnel department in many companies is changing. The task of selecting, training, identifying and motivating those with high potential is not a soft job. It is difficult . . . and potentially powerful. The personnel officer will need to be a futurist, someone thoroughly familiar with the company, its policies and structure, someone who can see precisely where a company is headed and where it needs to go. Instead of an unimpressive division, personnel can evolve into a center of real power and its director no longer a non-policy making VP, but a real contender for Chief Executive Officer. And some of the people who by their own initiative find themselves in that position, will be the women and minorities so many companies hired and didn't know what to do with.

———

The question is: how far do we in the U.S. have to be tested? The second World War tested us, Korea to an extent, the Cuban crisis. The question is really what is the mettle of the people today, the people that will lead to the future. I'm feeling a sort of inwardness from my students, a "me, myself, and I." People are retreating into home, family and occupation insofar as it provides for their needs rather than looking at the

world's problems. Now maybe this is a regeneration, but the retreat can move toward socialism and "take care of everything for me." ... When I really get uptight, I worry about the survival of capitalism.
—Ann Leven

If the baby boom produced the largest, most educated and change-oriented generation in this generation's history, it would seem to follow that the generation behind it—today's teenagers and college students—would produce an even better generation of forward-looking leaders. But something has already happened to that generation, a strong reaction to the intense competition in the previous one. In many ways, competition for jobs on the part of the baby boomers and an economy that, while responsive, cannot be responsive enough, has hit today's students. A combination of high population, a static economy and the desire for careers, not just jobs, has led to critical levels of youth unemployment. And some observers see the threat of social and political unrest that goes with such unemployment facing the world's industrialized democracies for years to come. In the U.S., where the youth unemployment rate hovers around 13 percent, the scenario is familiar: thousands of young people line up twelve hours ahead of time to apply for a handful of federally funded summer jobs. Most go away disappointed.

But it is not just America that faces such problems. The baby boom hit Canada and Europe, too. In the nine Common Market nations in Western Europe, unemployed young represent 37 percent of all unemployed—a hefty 2 million people. Official statistics in Italy say 36 percent of all youth there can't find jobs, but some observers say the more realistic figure is 65 percent. A Canadian government study states that college-trained workers will face intense competition for jobs until at least 1990. There are simply more young people than most economies can absorb and put to work for at least six years, perhaps fifteen if the world economy stays at present levels.

While the unemployment rate is doubled for minority youths, those among the traditionally "well-off" group—upper-middle- and upper-class Caucasians—are also feeling the pinch. Those who stay in school are under intense pressure. To see that, and to see how things have changed, one has to go no farther than Scarsdale High School in New York's affluent Westchester County. It has been called one of the finest public schools in the nation. Its students consistently score high on college entrance examinations and attend prestigious schools. Scarsdale High was a bastion of the rebellion of the Sixties, its students proudly wearing the badge of change under the guise of Sixties liberalism. In 1969 it gained some notoriety for presenting a summer school course in guerilla warfare so students could understand the Vietnam war. A visitor to Scarsdale High in 1978 would find some permanent changes wrought by the Sixties: the school newspaper estimates that 63 percent of the student body have tried marijuana and there is, according to students, an elevated level of sexual activity. But more revealing would be some startling changes in the other direction. The Scarsdale students of 1978 are not marching, innovating, protesting or even questioning, it seems. If anything, they are doing just the opposite. Influenced by the realities of an uncertain job market, cautious about the fate of the generation ahead of them, the high school students reflect what some observers say is a national trend: a return to the passivity, conformity and materialism of the 1950s. Instead of marching in front of the library, students are marching into it, to study for hours. Good grades have replaced good causes in their repertoire. Teachers report a high level of motivation and an intense desire to succeed in the real world.

Studious students, calm campuses, a renewed desire to succeed: all might seem too good to be true, and point toward a bright future. But within this "new" passivity and pragmatism, something has been lost. Observers, teachers and even parents of the prototypical Scarsdale High students worry that their young are too busy trying to reach for a good income and good place in life. The questioning that breeds an innovative mind has been seemingly forgotten. Like William Zinsser's Yale students who ask for a life plan at 18, the new young seem to be organizing their interests, time and energies around what other people expect of them, rather than what they themselves want. There is less group identity. Teachers are reporting a rise in cheating and plagiarism among students in order to achieve those all-important grades. The harsh realities of the economic situation have wrestled with traditional youthful values of questioning individuality and rebellion. The realities seem to have won.

And these realities are not to be found just in upper-class schools or high schools. Students—high school, college, or graduate—are by their very nature in a vulnerable and insecure position, faced with uncertainty and in need of a lot of luck. But today there seems to be an extra edge of insecurity for all of them, an almost desperate need to find one's secure job niche fast. Experimentation is out, hard facts are in, and those young successes who have observed what has happened are not too encouraged by it. Though young themselves, they speak of "these kids today" as though they were tribal elders—as in the success game they probably are. Ann Leven, who teaches MBA courses in addition to her job as treasurer of the Metropolitan Museum, speaks of the great insecurity her students seem to have inherited. She worries about her students opting for less desirable business situations because of their need for a secure job and good benefits. Such a trading off of power security, not the sole preserve of MBA students, has the potential to change life-styles and the professions. But such a tradeoff will not necessarily provide future leaders: one of the crucial factors for achievement and leadership is the willingness to take risks. With more people opting for security for its own sake, that risk orientation becomes increasingly rare.

Some, like Harvard professor Alan Dershowitz, see some good in the situation. When Dershowitz was going to law school in the early 1960s, he was representative of the early wave of baby boom generation lawyers: in looking for work after graduation, he and his colleagues basically had no hard-and-fast principles to compromise. One didn't think twice about going to a prestigious law firm. But the mid-Sixties changed all that. During the late Sixties and early Seventies, when radicals, turmoil and questioning had left their mark, Wall Street was no longer Mecca, but something to be avoided "on principle." Small public interest law firms were the "in" places to work, and students in many cases had rigid ideas of what was right, wrong and socially responsible. They were incapable of compromise. Today's law students, Dershowitz says, have a "healthy and realistic" attitude toward work. Realism exacts its toll even here—such students are torn and troubled at having to make explicit and realistic compromises in their choice of jobs. But compromise they do. While perhaps wanting, in spirit, to work for Ralph Nader, realistically the budding attorneys realize there is no future in it. Dershowitz believes that his students are still capable of changing their law firms for the good . . . if the guilt of making such compromises stays with them long enough.

A dependence on compromise guilt is not the most reliable —or encouraging—roadmap to the future. The willingness to compromise and opt for security that led to a comforting group-think in the 1950s, could be disastrous in the 1980s. An encouragement of such group-think on the part of a society that is manager- instead of leader-oriented dilutes individuality. This state of affairs has the early overachievers worried. They are not alone in their concern. To speak of the need for people with vision has a particular urgency to it in this decade. It is certainly vital for any society to have both leaders and followers—if every-one took an assertiveness course the result would be strife and chaos. Managers and leaders are both needed if society is to be kept on a smooth course.

But there are times of imbalance. Just as a desert is created when the climate changes and no rain falls for long periods of time, so a perpetual rainfall of group-think and manager-orienta-tion in business and cultural life can create a suffocating rain forest of inertia. Those who have made it young in America today have cleared a path in that rain forest. We could do worse than to take a few cues and some courage from them, in order to make a highway. The key to survival in such a situation is air. The key to growth is letting in some light. To make room for both requires difficult change, a rethinking of our institutions, how they function and an individual's place within them. The young success may be the last vestige of an old-fashioned work ethic in the present scheme of things, but he or she needn't become a relic. The responsibility of society to constructively encourage individuality has in lip service long been a national credo. With conviction, it could be our newest—and greatest—frontier.

# Epilogue

OUR FIRST REACTION when confronted with the complex subject of achieveing young in America might logically be to fear it. After all, the high-powered world of super success is foreign territory to most of us. What do we have in common with a law professor, a hotshot publisher, a rising corporate star? And since so many more of them seem to be around, does that mean we'll be trampled in the process? The new order, at first glance, appears to leave no room for average accomplishment. "Average" has fallen to the level of a negative term. This perceived new order, for many of us, is a frightening thing.

The second reaction to youth in power is discouragement. We are saturated by success reminders these days. Every day yet another new measure pops up to remind us we are/are not making it. If our salary doesn't equal or surpass our age, if our office is not a corner one, if we're not going through all the significant life passages our friends are going through—and at the proper age—

we feel left out. Books tell us how to dress to appear successful, what games to play and what lovers to avoid on our trip up. We look behind us and see young people zooming to the top. It's enough to make us want to bury our heads in sheer exasperation. The rules are swirling in a pool below us, and we're not sure where to jump in—or how.

Those are logical, initial reactions. After all, change—any change—is cause for hesitancy. The unknown is frightening, and corporate, cultural and social change imply uncharted territory. But as we've seen, the phenomenon of young success does not have to be terrifying or discouraging. It can enrich not only those who make it young, but also who don't. There are now choices for success. That attainment of a satisfying and happy personal life can be termed a major achievement just as much as being the president of one's own company. And because space at the top is limited, business today is faced with a responsibility to those who won't be moving up. The work place is paying more attention to the "average" worker, making an effort to show those employees who will remain at one level probably for the rest of their lives that they are needed and are making a valuable contribution. Our individual and corporate sensitivities are being sharpened.

What can we learn from young success? That those qualities needed to attain it are ones we each possess to some degree. That the ability to recognize an opportunity and to go one step further to risk-taking is a universal one, but one not universally exercised. That the ability to move on the dictates of one's inner clock, not that timetable followed by the rest of the population, is important. It's crucial to believe in one's instincts, and follow them. And when those instincts lead to failure, as they sometimes do, it's important to look back in order to apply the lessons learned. To dwell on a failure, however, sacrificing the present for the past, is counterproductive. Moving forward, whether one is aiming toward the boardroom or completion of an assembly-line task, will carry one into—and out of—the inevitable mistakes we each must make to change and grow.

And what is successful change? Thankfully, it has taken on new, individual meanings. One woman I know went through midlife career crisis at 26. A man I know went through it at age 60. She was twenty years early by the popular timetable, he twenty years late. These individuals are both successful people, but in different ways. She lives in a large city and has a fast-paced career which many might call glamorous. She travels constantly to exciting places, has a happy and hectic social life and is generally delighted with things. Yet she has already switched careers twice, and will probably go through more career changes as she gets older. He, on the other hand, lives in a smaller city, and has been teaching at a university there for many years. His is a slower kind of life, with little exotic travel and few exciting trappings—on the surface. But he is as vibrant, curious and growth-oriented as his jet-setting counterpart. At age 55 he took up playing the piano; at age 56 he wrote his first novel.

Both people are enjoying life. Both are welcoming change and growth, but in different ways. Both follow the young success pattern, only one is not in the conventional young-success age group. No matter. The problems and rewards are much the same, on different scales. Both worry about being sensitive to the people around them—she worries that her youth will threaten older coworkers; he worries that his age will put off younger coworkers. Their stories are not much different from young success stories in that both are moving forward, to destinations each truly wants. Each realizes that mistakes, failures and false starts are a part of the road to that individual destination.

The story of young success in America has one overriding theme, and that is the value of individual decision and desire. Young achievers are setting the tone for the way we conduct our business, cultural and social lives. And they are doing it because they follow their own passages, not someone else's. They seem to be telling us that if you want to stay in middle management and move no higher, then don't become a Peter Principle statistic just because someone says you should aim for the boardroom. They are telling us, if you are bright and young—or bright and older—you have every right to question why you're not moving toward the boardroom fast enough. If you're ambitious, they are saying, then don't be ashamed of it. And, conversely, don't be embarrassed if you simply want an uncomplicated life free of stressful success-striving.

As a result of the Sixties, the definitions of success are many. Those who rise quickly to the top of the conventional ladder are certainly accomplished. But equally successful are those who choose willingly not to. There is room for both—and for infinite variations in between.

# Index